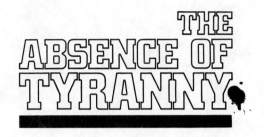

THE ABSENCE OF TYRANNY

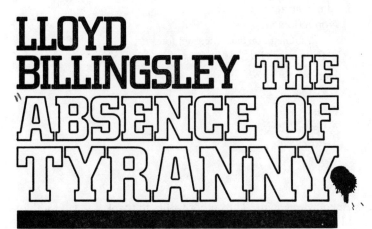

LLOYD BILLINGSLEY

"THE ABSENCE OF TYRANNY

Recovering Freedom in Our Time

MULTNOMAH · PRESS

Portland, Oregon 97266

By the same author:
Nonfiction:
   The Generation that Knew not Josef
   Religion's Rebel Son: Fanaticism in Our Time
Fiction:
   A Year for Life
Plays:
   Green Card
   Royal Suite

Acknowledgments: The author wishes to thank Randall Kuhl for his assistance in the preparation of this book.

Edited by Rodney L. Morris
Cover design by Larry Ulmer

THE ABSENCE OF TYRANNY
©1986 by Lloyd Billingsley
Published by Multnomah Press
Portland, Oregon 97266

Printed in the United States of America

Library of Congress Cataloging-in-Publication Data

Billingsley, Lloyd.   # 13665796
   The absence of tyranny.

   Bibliography p.
   Includes index.
   1. Liberty. 2. Ideology. I. Title.
JC585.B52   1986   320'.01'1   86-13149
ISBN 0-88070-166-8

86 87 88 89 90 91 – 10 9 8 7 6 5 4 3 2 1

51458

For M

CONTENTS

FOREWORD

Lloyd Billingsley can tell the difference between moralism and morality from a mile away, at least. The first is the posturing of self-righteousness, the second is the quest for approximate good in a world of pervasive evil. With an engaging mix of clarity, passion, and whimsy, this book pleads with us to accept a measure of moral responsibility for the future of freedom in the world. Only a measure of responsibility, to be sure, for the future of freedom is finally not in our hands. In the Christian view of things, freedom is God's gift and, by his grace, the destiny of humankind.

There are things we can and should do, however. We can be grateful for freedom and sing its blessings. We can recommend it to others and in full awareness of our fallibility, make prudential judgments about policies that can enhance freedom here and abroad. And there are things we can and should stop doing. Above all, we should stop the moralistic posturing that pits "freedoms" (economic, psychological, sexual, and on and on) against freedom. Billingsley is especially effective when he exposes such posturing, but this book is much more than a polemic. Only the careless reader will fail to see that the incisive (and necessary) criticism emerges from the author's profound affirmation of the wonder and fragility of freedom in the political orders of the world. Billingsley knows what Christians too often forget: that perfect freedom awaits the consummation of history in

the establishment of the Kingdom of God. Short of that—
and we are very much short of that—we walk by faith, making our decisions in the courage of uncertainty and confi-
dence in the forgiveness that is greater than our errors.

Billingsley also knows that the understanding of freedom begins with the negative, just as the divine commandments begin with the "thou shalt nots." With respect to the
power of the state and other overweening structures of the
present time, the first commandment of freedom is, "Thou
shalt not coerce thy neighbor's mind or soul." Put positively,
that means freedom of conscience, and freedom of the most
sacred precinct of conscience, which is freedom of religion.
One of the most striking signs of apostasy in our day is the
readiness of church people and church institutions to subor-
dinate freedom of religion to "rights" associated with the
satisfaction of material needs. The irony, of course, is that
where freedom of mind and soul is denied, all other freedoms, real and alleged, are also frustrated. That ironic consequence has been demonstrated again and again in this century's experience with sundry "socialisms" and "liberationisms."

To be sure, it is not only under regimes of the Left that
freedom is repressed, and Billingsley might be criticized for
not addressing equal attention to the denial of freedom by
regimes of the Right. To that criticism at least three responses are in order. First, there is no worldwide network of
the Right aggressively bent upon the denial of freedom. On
the Left, so to speak, there is. It is called Marxist-Leninism.
Second, regimes on the Right are devoted to maintaining
themselves in power, not to controlling the entire society.
Only Marxist-Leninism today is in principle committed to
the totalitarian maxim first proposed by Mussolini, "Everything for the state, nothing against the state, nothing outside the state." Third, the friends of unfreedom in the prestige
cultural, educational, and religious leadership circles of our
society are, as it happens, overwhelmingly on the Left.

In addition, the responsible person tries to keep things

in perspective. The likes of Mussolini and Hitler are dead, along with their movements. Wherever their ideas may be revived, they must be condemned and nipped in the bud. Marxist-Leninism, however, despite its consistent record of producing human misery, is alive and well—especially among some "radical" Christians who have lately come upon its tired and tattered ideas with a sense of fresh discovery. Were it not so sad, it would be amusing to see "socialist Christians" and "Christian socialists," like the generals who plan to fight the last war, promulgating the "new" ideas that have served the cause of unfreedom so long and so ingloriously. These ideas too have consequences, and it is obvious to all but the willfully blind that those consequences are massive and lethal. In the 1950s Senator Joseph McCarthy and his allies inadvertently turned "anti-communism" into a dirty word. Today those who are truly pledged to liberal democracy must rediscover their nerve in an unabashed declaration of anti-communism. Anti-communism, it should be made very clear, is not a sufficient political philosophy, but it is a necessary presupposition for admission to the company of the friends of freedom.

Finally, in the course of his lively argument Billingsley makes some definite proposals for how the world might be reordered. I confess to finding some of them more provocative than persuasive. But all of them serve to open up new avenues of discussion about what it means to be a free society, and about moral responsibility for expanding the community of democratic peoples. The late John Courtney Murray, the great Catholic proponent of liberal democracy, was fond of saying that in discussion we should seek both agreement and disagreement. Disagreement, he believed, is a rare and valuable commodity. Most of what is called disagreement, Father Murray said, is really just confusion. The reader of this important book may be led to agreement with Billingsley at many points. But it is no little achievement if the reader is also led through confusion to disagreement. In either case, the cause of clarity is served and we are all better equipped to accept our share of moral responsibility for the future of freedom in the world.

Richard John Neuhaus
Director
The Rockford Institute Center
  on Religion and Society
New York City

Resolved, in all circumstances, to live and die a free man. No tyranny, however odious, no warfare, however destructive, can prevent this. It is what I will do.

Malcolm Muggeridge

¿Le Gusta Este Jardín?
¿Que Es Suyo?
¡Evite Que Sus Hijos Lo Destruyan! *

A sign in Mexico, recorded in Malcolm
Lowry's *Under the Volcano*

*Do you like this garden?
Is it yours?
Prevent your children from destroying it!

INTRODUCTION

We have now sunk to a depth at which the restatement of
the obvious is the first duty of intelligent men.

George Orwell

Nothing is so treacherous as the obvious.

Joseph Schumpeter

At a recent writers conference prospective scribes,
with pens at the ready and cassette recorders on full alert,
packed into a workshop to hear a best-selling author of inspi-
rational books reveal the secrets of the trade. He told the
eager troops that the first step in authoring any piece of literature was to establish their "platform," that is, their authority on the chosen subject. There is considerable merit in
this advice, particularly if one were to undertake a treatise
on quantum physics, a study of the sexual habits of Tibetans,
or a Swahili-Finnish lexicon. Who would publish, much less
buy, such a thing if it were done by, say, Tip O'Neill? But
the subject of freedom must remain open to the masses; it is
not only for politicians and philosophers, but for everyone.

Most philosophical questions are really, at bottom,
religious ones capable of being grasped by secretaries, plow-
men, and grade school teachers in any country of the world
at any time. Similarly, in the present Age of Politics most if
not all political questions deal in principle with freedom or
its absence. Part of my purpose is to stimulate discussion of

these issues not just in the isolation wards of the academy and the seminary but, as they say in Quebec, in *le grand public*. And like it or not, everyone is included; agnostics, Christians, Jews, hedonists, feminists, neo-Luddites, urban communards, electronic evangelists, electronic engineers—everyone. This being so, it is of great concern that both freedom and truth have been practically discarded by many of those who are supposed to be their guardians. Social Justice, not freedom, is today's pursuit.

This book represents what I want to say about freedom. It is not, in the popular sense of the term, "prophetic," which is often a shortcut to a platform of authority as well as a clever way of placing the wildest of pronouncements beyond the pale of examination. The technique works rather well.

This author claims no infallibility of any sort. It is indeed possible that I have made a great mistake in advocating liberty. All those opposed to freedom are hereby invited to write a book refuting this one and showing how the absence of freedom furthers peace, justice, the abundance of food, human rights, the pursuit of happiness, philanthropy, and all the other good things to which people through the ages have dedicated their lives. If anyone can convince me that freedom is an evil, and that God is very much against it, I will publicly renounce this book. They can even call their stance prophetic if they like. I don't mind.

I took no mystical dictation, saw no visions, and neither received the message on stone tablets nor dug it up in the form of golden plates. Neither do I have a doctorate in freedom. The only authority I can claim is that I am a free person and intend to remain so. Hence, this is not an authoritarian work in the sense desired by the best-selling author mentioned earlier, the rest of whose talk, I should add, was pure Freshman Composition..

But while angelic intervention was absent in the preparation of this work, so were visits from any secret police force. I followed my usual practice and wrote exactly what I pleased. All my research material—subversive stuff like the

Bible, *The Wealth of Nations,* and Gertrude Himmelfarb's *Victorian Minds,* among others—was readily available. So were *Das Kapital* and a host of other works that advocate the violent overthrow of liberal democracy. I needed no internal passport or permission of any kind to go wherever I pleased to complete my work. Once finished, I had no obligation to submit the manuscript to censors or party officials of any persuasion. It was not rejected on the grounds that I do not belong to any political party. There are no canons of Capitalist Realism, Corporate Realism, or Socialist Realism on which its publication depended. Under present conditions, there is no chance that I will be deported or jailed for setting forth my case in a public forum.

These freedoms are the basic working conditions of a writer, and they are absent in much of the world. Anyone who thinks that such bourgeois trifles are unimportant is demanding his own destruction—alas, a common malaise in our time. Part of my purpose is to pay respect to the system of liberty, and those responsible for it, that makes these bourgeois trifles possible. I am aware that many consider this a sort of romantic *déjà vu* for an age that is passing away. To this I can only say that such *déjà vu* is much to be preferred over *presque vu,* and is a clear winner over *jamais vu.*[1]

Although I do not consider freedom the highest value (if it were, a prison would be the greatest evil), it is what makes any meaningful activity in life possible. It allows us to exercise our beliefs, our conscience, to choose between good and evil, to select our associations. Far from being a mere philosophical concept, it is the very foundation of civilized society. Without this liberty, in fact, there can be no true society at all, or even true human beings . . . just a congregation of clever, tool-using animals, herded or stampeded about by Great Helmsmen Who Know What's Best For Everyone.

Moreover, for what it is worth, I not only intend to remain a free person but will do everything in my power to insure that my children (and yours) and their children remain free. Although a guardian only of my own freedom, I will also be a promoter of liberty everywhere, and urge others to do the same. That these stands, once common, and the people who make them are now readily labeled "controversial" or worse only makes the case for a book like this stronger.

But what, exactly, is freedom? This is an involved and currently confused subject since nobody can be found to speak against it in principle. Hugh Hefner, the animal rights crusaders, appliance manufacturers, and many other disparate groups and individuals all claim freedom as their cause. Even Pol Pot, the Wayne Gretzky of modern genocide, sees himself as a liberator. We can't all be talking about the same thing.

What I mean by freedom will be outlined in the rest of this book, but let me say at the outset that freedom is primarily an absence and not a presence. It is freedom *from* before freedom *to*. The second depends on the first. For this very reason, freedom bears a considerable rhetorical handicap. Those to whom it is important sometimes turn to anecdotes to explain what they mean.

When Malcolm Muggeridge left the Soviet Union in 1933, the instant his train passed through the border into a then independent Latvia, all the passengers burst into cheers and shouts. They looked back at the guards and triumphantly shook their fists. "We were out," Muggeridge wrote, "we were free."[2] Former United States Treasury Secretary William E. Simon reports a similar spontaneous demonstration when the plane carrying his delegation lifted off from the Moscow airport. "I understood down to my very roots," he says, "how important my liberty was to me, that the need for it was part of my very identity."[3] Three young Cubans who recently floated to Florida on inner tubes surely felt the same way.[4] There are many such stories and they all say to me with one voice, "Free at last! Thank God I'm free at last!"

My feelings on the subject were once crystallized by a relative who had to endure the privations of a particularly obtuse socialist regime whose reign was mercifully brief. He had received a notice by mail informing him that an industry with which he was only remotely connected—as a customer, actually—had been suddenly "nationalized." He had fought in World War II and knew that freedom can be taken away, but now a dimension of his own had been eliminated. Furthermore, it was tersely demanded of him: "You shall appear personally" at a specific place and time for further instructions. I asked how he responded to this summons; he replied without hesitation: "I immediately said to myself, *I shall not.*" This stance seems to me entirely proper and healthy, the more so since legions of authoritarian politicians and clergy would dub this man "reactionary," or even "dangerous," and in a way I suppose he is. Not that this is a bad thing at This Stage of History.

By now it should be generally apparent what we are talking about: freedom as the absence of tyranny. This is the starting point. If the reader finds this concept archaic ("nineteenth-century bourgeois individualism"), illusory, simplistic, or distasteful, and would prefer instead some psychological semantics or a spirited defense of contemporary serfdom, let her immediately return this volume to the bookseller or the library shelf. She will find much in both places that will be of great comfort and encouragement.

But since the subject of freedom is as wide as existence itself and touches a number of subjects that various disciplines claim as their private turf, there will be protests. "Here is some scribbler," they will say, "who quotes a lot of people who are old or dead, assembles a few outdated ideas he finds lying around a library, then proceeds to tell us what to think."

The only defense a writer can offer to this common complaint is that this is the nature of his profession, but not his alone. As Evelyn Waugh pointed out in the foreword to *Robbery Under Law,*[5] many a lawyer meets with a client over cocktails and smoked salmon, skims his notes and legal briefs in the afternoon, then pleads the case in court as though it had been the central quest of his life, and the defendant dearer to him than his own mother. He then cashes his fat check and instantly forgets everything about his customer, whose innocence or guilt is quite often a matter of indifference to him.

Similarly, a physician sees a previously unknown woman for a few minutes, tells her to disrobe, pokes around with his fingers, taps with a hammer, peers into orifices with a flashlight, scans a few charts, then prescribes some drugs or treatment. The next day he bills Medicare but, while driving home in his BMW, may well be hard pressed to remember what his patient looked like.

It is the writer's business to observe, investigate, interpret, record, then publish his findings. The critical and commercial marketplace are his ultimate judges. There is a public dimension to his work absent from other professions. (How many doctors have their surgical technique held up to public display on television? How many lawyers' closing arguments or professors' lectures are reviewed by John Simon in *Esquire?*) In writing about freedom I am just doing my job, which, at This Stage of History, happens to be a kind of translation.

With apologies to the few remaining devotees of Esperanto,[6] the universal language of this age is Newspeak. In this cant dialect, all important words have meanings that are often the exact opposite of their traditional sense. For example, the slogan of INGSOC (English Socialism) in *1984*, FREEDOM IS SLAVERY, is pretty much what many people mean by the term today. Unfortunately, it is easier to translate into Newspeak than out, but it must be done. The reader should consider this book a sort of Newspeak-English dictionary. And there is another analogy that is appropriate.

One remembers the delightful scene in Annie Hall when Woody Allen and Diane Keaton are exchanging small talk on a New York balcony and the real meaning is given in subtitles. Whenever Newspeak orators hold forth—in classrooms, on television screens, and, increasingly, in pulpits and seminaries—someone must supply subtitles or the audience will remain hopelessly confused, even lost. Allen's vignette was of course hilarious, true *cinéma vérité*. Humor, particularly satire, deals with the gap between what people are and what they proclaim to be, between pretension and reality, rhetoric and meaning. I want to train people to write their own subtitles.

Finally, a modern writer is not only a translator and subtitler, but is necessarily conscripted into salvage operations. The present is fleeting, the future uncertain. Anyone who writes on freedom must plunge deep into the past, which is really all we have. And just as Jacques Cousteau's divers in search of some sunken archeological treasure are occasionally menaced by sharks or toothy moray eels, there are also clear dangers on these spiritual and intellectual recovery missions. The currents of ideological fashion are stronger than anything in the ocean. Here I speak from experience.

A progressive gentleman connected with the book trade was "deeply saddened" that in an earlier volume[7] I had been less than worshipful of religious socialists, past and present. In fact, I was and still am quite critical of them, just as Ralph Nader is critical of corporations, none of which, by the way, is as large as the Methodist Church or has a periodical with a circulation as wide as *Sojourners*. Mr. Nader is positively revered by the media for his "watchdog" and "consumer advocate" roles, to the point that he is invited to be guest host on "Saturday Night Live." Even if being a critic of Christian socialists brings no such rewards, it is a legitimate activity since it is concerned with multi-national manufacturers of an ideology that threatens the freedom of everyone. It is a consumer safety issue.

I committed the great sin of telling my readers just who I was talking about and why. If this was not bad enough, I even quoted from their published articles and books. ("Yes, your honor, I did it. I confess.") It was surely an unprecedented offense that will be repeated in this volume.

Corporation bashers like Ralph Nader and Mr. Tom Fonda would never cite *actual data* in their arguments against nuclear power and the Corvair, would they? A court-appointed lawyer defending a Hispanic welfare mother charged with murder would surely never stoop so low as to call living witnesses?

In any case, what I did was unacceptable to this would-be literary arbiter who apparently thought I should have protected these people from themselves by explaining what they thought they meant, instead of commenting on what they actually wrote. My book "never should have been published," he said with unusual candor, displaying sentiments that would fit right in with the publishing philosophy of Albania.

The point is, there is a lobby of statist opinion—particularly in the religious world—that resists traditional ideas of freedom. This entrenched New Class still sets the agenda and proclaims: "These areas are our specialty. You shall go to the back of the bus and be quiet."

I shall not.

INTRODUCTION, NOTES

1. *Déjà vu* means "already seen," *presque vu* "nearly seen," and *jamais vu* "never seen."
2. Malcolm Muggeridge, *The Green Stick*, vol. 1 (New York: William Morrow, 1973), 267.
3. William E. Simon, *A Time for Truth* (New York: McGraw-Hill, 1978), 18.
4. "Three Cubans Rescued Off Coast of Florida," Los Angeles Times, 1 August 1985, sec. 1.
5. The book deals with Mexican nationalization of the oil industry and is highly recommended. It is published in the United States by Little, Brown under the title, *Mexico: An Object Lesson*.
6. Esperanto is an artificial language invented by Russian linguist Dr. L. Zamenhof in 1887. At one time it was hoped that it would become the international lingua franca and break down barriers between the peoples of the world; a reversal of the Tower of Babel, as it were. To its rapidly dwindling devotees it is a linguistic hobby. To statesmen it is only an intellectual curiosity.
7. Lloyd Billingsley, *The Generation that Knew Not Josef*, (Portland, Ore.: Multnomah Press, 1985).

PART

1

FREEDOM

CHAPTER 1
OBSTACLES TO A DISCUSSION OF FREEDOM

THE WORD RECOGNITION GAME

Let any public official of conservative inclinations use the word *freedom* in a speech and it is guaranteed to elicit a negative emotional reaction in a good percentage of the audience. In fact, one sometimes hears hoots of derision on such occasions. The term has come to be associated with a certain political atavism. Whatever particular definition the hearer might have for the word, he is certain that the speaker's version of freedom is a belch from the past, and largely fraudulent. This negative imagery is supplied in bulk by popular culture.

In the film *Coming Home*, for example, a soldier makes a speech to his fellow veterans. He is old and frail, an image of dusty tradition and patriotism straight from central casting. In halting speech, he expresses gratitude that, during one military campaign in Europe, he was "able to participate in the liberation of many towns." At this point we cut to a young, black Vietnam veteran being wheeled by on a gurney. He hears the speaker's comment, looks momentarily cynical, then flashes the time-out sign. It may not seem like it, but there is a lot going on here. This scene manages to convey, with only a few lines of dialogue, the following proposition: "The whole notion of freedom as something worth fighting for died with the last generation. Why, just look at the waste and misery this idea causes in the present, now that we have all come of age." It is a brilliant piece of didactic filmmaking.

Another movie, *The Candidate*, deals with an American election. The "traditional" politician who spouts a lot of clichés about freedom is older, slightly obese, and certainly on the greasy side. It is made clear that this man is a toady of big business, and he is also shown joining with football players in a pregame prayer. On the other hand, the idealistic young liberal, played by Robert Redford, is a dashing, sartorially resplendent messiah of the downtrodden and oppressed. Beautiful women throw themselves at him. This clever use of appearance and style is like the look-see reading method of modern grade schools. This is look-see political consciousness raising:

> "See the fat, ugly, evil man. See how he talks of freedom, when he is really a pawn of Big Money. See how he prays just so people will see him. Look how phony he is. Now see the good man. He wants to help others. See how pretty he is! See how everyone loves him. Which one do you want to be like?"

This of course is a variation on the old white hats (good guys) versus black hats (bad guys) theme, which, in fact, is still used. In the spy thriller, *Hopscotch*, with Walter Mathau and Glenda Jackson, the CIA man wears a black hat; likewise the strike breakers in Warren Beatty's *Reds*—a long piece of hagiography about journalist John Reed.[1]

Many other examples come to mind, especially from that electronic pedagogue for the subliterate, television. There, the few people who care for freedom are bigoted Archie Bunkers or Ebenezer Scrooge types who snarl, "there is no free lunch" and gripe about pinko liberals who "never met a payroll."

As Irving Kristol and others have pointed out, ours is the first civilization whose popular culture is at odds with the values and ideas of the civilization itself—particularly freedom. It is as if some determined marine biologist, after years of work, was finally able to get an erudite dolphin to talk, and listened in horror to a denunciation of air and water, the very elements in which the creature lives and on which its life depends.

In mass culture, "Freedom's just another word for nothing left to lose," as Kris Kristofferson puts it in the song "Bobby McGee." In other words, freedom's just another word for nothing meaningful at all. So why bother with it?

One exception to the above is country-western music and its singers who are not embarrassed by freedom. But this is taken as confirmation that freedom is a "redneck" or "fundy" sentiment, held by people with southern accents who drive pick-up trucks. New Class[2] academics, clergy, and media people would rather be photographed slinking out of a showing of *Deep Throat*, clinging to a prostitute and swigging wine from a bottle in a paper bag, than be associated with the political views of, say, Merle Haggard. The association of freedom with such (to them) disreputable types is often enough to cause its rejection out of sheer peer pressure. The modern New Class intellectuals, like medieval monks, try to get as far away from the blue-collar herd as possible.

Another reason for freedom's rhetorical handicap is the use of the word *liberty* by extremist anti-Semitic groups. Liberty Lobby, for example, is an organization dedicated to disproving Hitler's genocide against European Jews, which they contend never happened.[3] They view the holocaust as a gigantic hoax invented and maintained by Jews to extort money and support for the state of Israel. The whole thrust of this and similar groups is anti-Semitic. Their world view is that of a conspiracy of international bankers (a code word for Jews) who rule the world. The entire American political system does exactly what these people tell them, so the theory goes. These dog-eared fantasies have nothing to do with political theory but are pure demonology. There is no evidence that those who hold them have any affection for political freedom and cultural pluralism at all. But groups like this cover themselves with a confetti of words like *liberty*, *historical review*, and *labor*. Unfortunately, this kind of verbal theft for purposes of propaganda has caused freedom to be regarded with suspicion. Worse still, it has added to it a whiff of conspiracy.

Besides extremist groups, special interest lobbies like the National Rifle Association distribute bumper stickers that read "NRA Freedom." Without getting into the merits and claims of this, suffice it to say that groups like the NRA are regularly lampooned in popular culture as congregations of social neanderthals whose highest value is the right to own and operate an M-16 assault rifle in any way they see fit. Even if the caricature of these people is false, as it no doubt is, and even if their use of the term *freedom* is legitimate, the very currency of the word is devalued in the popular mind by the association with guns. Neither God nor freedom are the sort of thing you honk for, but they nevertheless find their way onto bumper stickers and T-shirts. The result is that when one uses the word *freedom* in a political discussion, a kind of trigger-happy cowboy image can easily come to mind.

About the only time freedom is celebrated in song, apart from country music, is in national anthems. Canadians sing of the "true north strong and free," and Americans of "the land of the free." Since this happens mostly at sporting events, teary-eyed commemoration of one's political liberties comes to be associated with professional athletics and their fans. Since there are untold thousands of games each year, most of them meaningless, the anthems of freedom can easily be viewed as redundant, or at least become common. Then too there are names like the Freedom Bowl and Liberty Bowl. The word *freedom* becomes part of an often repeated and boring ceremony to be got out of the way before the action starts. This author can think of no good reason for the singing of national anthems at sporting events. It may be stretching things, but I believe that this too has helped to dull or confuse an important issue.

So has the use of the word *freedom* by advertisers. It has been emblazoned in huge Ben-Hur letters on a 7-11 store near my house. There is a Delco "Freedom" battery and "Stay-Free" tampons. What advertisers are selling is convenience. Now, it is a wonderful thing to toss dirty clothes into an automatic machine rather than wash them by hand in the local creek, but convenience is not the same as freedom. Somehow, "convenience" doesn't cut it in neon lights; it is far more appealing to promise the buyer freedom, especially when the asylums are full and many people don't "feel" free. The widespread use of the term *freedom* in advertising both dulls the edges of the concept and hatches another set of misleading associations.

The currency of freedom in its traditional sense has thus been so debased through overuse, neglect, caricature, and deliberate propaganda, that one finds academics and serious writers who can barely use the term without putting it in quotes. Sometimes a journalistic sneer is added, as in "the so-called free world,"[4] or our "so-called freedoms." By these the speaker means those bourgeois trifles referred to earlier—meaningless, abstract, phantasmagorical stuff such as open elections, freedom of the press, of enterprise, speech, religion, emigration and so on. Who in his right mind, the argument goes, wouldn't trade these gossamers for the Full Employment and Security supplied by an omnipotent government? Although academics, artists, and intellectuals, in particular, depend on these "formal" freedoms for their very livelihood, they are nevertheless often scorned as "so-called." Psychologist Rollo May gauges whether a political candidate is a "reactionary" by the number of times he uses the word *freedom* in a speech.[5]

Any work on freedom must recognize this rhetorical handicap at the outset. Just as a National Socialist Berliner in 1938 would have felt guilty for being kind to a rabbi, or may have perhaps referred to him as a "so-called human being," many today cannot say a kind word about freedom or make an unqualified reference to it without embarrassment.

The social, professional, and psychological costs are often too high.

FREE SPIRITS AND THE PURSUIT OF HAPPINESS

> Men are qualified for civil liberty in exact proportion to
> their disposition to put moral chains on their appetites.
> Edmund Burke

> Freedom is not only the absence of external restraint. It
> is also the absence of irresistible internal compulsions,
> unmanageable passions, and uncensorable appetites.
> George F. Will

Television sports announcers will occasionally comment about an athlete who spends much of his time in bars, much of his money on chemical recreation, and much of his energy chasing the ladies. Though such ones have recently been jailed for drug offenses, they are often referred to as "free spirits." (The rare athlete who stays at home and reads philosophy is sometimes tagged a "flake.") This is another example of the equation of liberty with license.

Classical liberalism is composed of those doctrines which pertain to free people. In a liberal society, people are free to do as they please, but, as Burke put it, what will it please them to do? The principle of freedom is fine; what about the performance of the individuals in its domains? Does that affect anything?

We all enjoy denouncing the sins of the gangster-statesmen of our time, such as Hitler, Mao Tse-tung, and Pol Pot. It is fatuously easy to do so, since most of us will never be in a position to give orders on which the lives of millions depend. But none of us is perfect, and all of us have the potential for such evil. With apologies to certain television preachers, we need no one to inform us of the misdeeds we actually commit; we know them all too well. "I struggle with that," we say, meaning, "I know the problem, but I'm not doing too much about it." In each human heart there is a ruthless politburo of desire, whose propaganda department, under the headline of Freedom, issues manifestos such as this: "I do whatever I want." This sounds like it lines up with freedom of the most laissez-faire type, but that is not the case.

Doing whatever one wants, or getting what one wants, is not freedom, yet even religious writers describe it that way.

> The dominant conservative outlook is that the future should be left not to state planners but to the free market mechanism. They genuinely believe that a system in which all people are *free to get as much as they can for themselves* will work for the common good.[6] (Italics added)

The freedom of the free market, as will be seen, is freedom *from* state coercion not, as this writer has it, getting as much as you can. In a free system, there are plenty of checks on individuals "getting as much as they can for themselves"—the existence of other people, laws, prices, and public demand.

Without a sense of responsibility and a well-defined moral code, doing or getting what one wants can easily lead to servitude, not to mention the actual harm it causes. It is interesting that the most extreme sexual libertines, "swingers" who are supposedly "free" from the "repressive" Judeo-Christian past, take great delight in such sadistic practices as "bondage." The use of this word is no accident; it is a shining example of the fearful symmetry that William Blake saw everywhere.

I remember reading about a divorced woman who was trying very hard to maintain a household and raise her family, but spent, by her own admission, far too much time in singles' bars and various men's beds to attain her goals. Her life was a mess, but she nonetheless always found herself "wanting to party." Her analyst, after exhausting numerous strategies, finally told her, "Look, you don't have to do what you want." I don't know how her case turned out; she may be a go-go dancer somewhere. Perhaps she got things under control. I hope so.

A free person does not have to do what he wants to do. Our inner politburo of desire is relentless, noisy, and staffed with skillful liars; like other politburos, it does not have our good in mind. But it can be defied and resisted with impunity.

I request that the non-Christian reader, particularly an academic, forgive me for mentioning Jesus Christ. I realize he is, after all, a sociological nonstarter. What books did he read? How did he vote? What schools did he attend? What awards and grants did he gain? His comments on personal freedom and morality are not technical but certainly come right to the point: "Whoever commits sin," Christ says, "is the servant of sin" (John 8:34). Likewise, the Old Testament supplies object lessons of how moral license leads not only to personal servitude, but collective servitude. Whenever the Israelites abandoned God for idolatry, which was accompanied by all kinds of licentiousness and even child sacrifice, they were swiftly taken over by a neighbor nation and forced to work as slaves. The loss of true personal freedom leads to the loss of collective freedom.

Nowhere in this book will it be contended that a free society is possible without morals, without virtue, without responsibility, without free consciences. A free market alone is not enough, particularly when many entrepreneurs look on moral aberrations and nihilism in terms of new business opportunities. Montesquieu observed that the English had done remarkably well in three important things: commerce, freedom, and piety. (Remarkably generous comments about the English for a Frenchman.) Max Weber comments on this observation: "Is it not possible that their commercial superiority and their adaptations to free political institutions are connected in some way with that record of piety?"[7] One would certainly think so. Jefferson adds:

> And can the liberties of a nation be thought secure when we have removed their only firm basis, a conviction in the minds of the people that these liberties are the gift of God?[8]

People who believe that human beings are the result of a long process of nothing plus time plus chance equals life and complexity, have great difficulty with the idea of freedom as a gift of God. But we won't get into that here.

In truth, the family, not the individual, is the fundamental unit of a free society. Moral license breaks down the family, and, hence, society as well. Can we expect those who cheat on their wife or husband to be honest in business, or in paying their taxes, or in obeying the law?

"Free as a bird," is a common expression. And yet, the freedom of birds is limited by gravity, atmospheric conditions, and the laws of aerodynamics. The author of the poem "High Flight" speaks of regions where neither lark nor eagle fly. So too are there limitations to human freedom. Absolute freedom is a meaningless slogan.

Moral license is really bondage, a bogus freedom that finds many takers, with heads thrust deeply in the trough. Politicians and activists of statist inclinations, whose self-image is such that they call themselves civil libertarians without any embarrassment, seldom oppose moral license because it gives the illusion of freedom to the very people they are slowly bureaucratizing into serfdom. This kind of moral laissez-faire, not traditional religion, is the true opium of the people. Proponents of an omnipotent state would like citizens to imagine that their freedom is enhanced because they can legally buy pornography or watch live sex shows and snuff films. But under such conditions, attitudes toward civic freedom itself deteriorate, as Robert Nisbet observed:

> Civic freedom comes to be detested by widening numbers of people when its fruits are more likely to be decaying ones of freely exhibited obscenity and morally irresponsible demands than those which the greater philosophers of individual freedom intended.[9]

What the greater philosophers of freedom such as Edmund Burke, Adam Smith, J.S. Mill, and the American constitutional framers had in mind was not the freedom to market obscenities, but freedom to engage in enterprise, philanthropy, the political process, and many other concerns. They took for granted a Judeo-Christian social ethic

and a strong family unit, which have been under heavy attack by ideological nerve gas for more than a century.

The detestation of civic freedom Nisbet refers to is in
itself an interesting question: How do people who enjoy all
the benefits of a free society come to scorn political freedom
itself? Why do they call the highest political values, for
which many people have died, our "so-called freedoms"?
The process has a peculiar methodology, but one must back
up a bit first.

One of the most disastrous phrases of all time is the
"pursuit of happiness." Pascal observed that in making happiness our goal, we insure that we will never attain it.
Nevertheless, Americans are constitutionally obliged to pursue it and do so with the same determination that the NRA
shows in clinging tenaciously to its right to bear arms. Witness the daily stampede to "happy hours" in bars. Whatever
definition of "happiness" one chooses (it is often equated
with sexual fulfillment), or whatever one thinks of the possibilities of its attainment, it should be noted that in a free
society one is entitled only to the *pursuit* of happiness. It is
now fashionable to take things much farther. Ronald
Berman points out that, to many a contemporary mind, "we
are not alone entitled to the pursuit of happiness, but to its
actual capture."[10]

But all the various avenues to happiness—especially
sex—often turn out to be blind alleys that lead only to satiety
and disgust, what Malcolm Muggeridge called the "death
camp of carnality." So weak are many people's religious, political, and philosophical principles—if they have any at
all—that they have practically abandoned the life of the
mind altogether and now depend heavily on sentimentality
and sensation. They let their feelings rather than their mind
or conscience be their guide. "How do you *feel* about that,
Basil?" says the therapist. Chesterton says, "This is a psychological age, which is the opposite of an intellectual age."[11]

Former vice-presidential candidate Geraldine Ferraro,
while flogging Pepsi on television, informs us that, "what's

right is what feels right." Statements like this make me regret that she was not elected. We might have been treated to a White House press conference like this:

> *Diane Sawyer*: Vice-president Ferraro, in your opinion, does the new immigration bill outline a fair strategy for the country?
>
> *Vice-president Ferraro*: (muses a moment) Well, Diane, what's right is what feels right.

This standard of right and wrong would have surprised Aristotle, Martin Luther King, and probably even Karl Marx, though the Marquis de Sade might have agreed. "What's right is what feels right," is no basis for personal ethics, much less a foundation for a free society.

All human feelings are notoriously unpredictable and cannot be maintained at levels of "happiness," (Are 3.47 zigrafs of happiness acceptable? Or can one get by with 2.51?) even with the use of chemicals, legal or illegal. And even if someone should happen to describe their happiness as "feeling free," this sensation is not likely to last long. The most libidinous womanizer, locked for a month in a motel with seven voluptuous (attention, feminists) "playmates" would most likely emerge not satisfied, "free" and "happy," but frustrated and jaded, and perhaps also possessed of some exotic disease. That most astute observer of societies, Alexis de Tocqueville, noted that in democracies, even in the midst of abundance, a "strange melancholy" and a "feeling of disgust" was often the lot of the common citizen.[12] Even the most free, most prosperous societies lie well east of Eden.

But here things get interesting. Too many people, when they discover that they are not "happy" or do not "feel free," conclude that they are politically *oppressed*. They do not consider that the problem lies within themselves but claim to be victims of free political institutions which, in their thinking, have not only failed to deliver the requisite results or feelings, but are held to be the ultimate *cause* of the unhappiness. As a non sequitur, this is surely one of the most perverse of all time, but it is widespread.

Sociologists in search of a subject or a grant see great possibilites in these attitudes, especially since the social sciences are, increasingly, political sciences. Sociologists of a religious bent are prone to take reality—imperfection in all its manifestations—as a proof text for utopian schemes. Bureaucrats, who would implement such schemes, are always thrilled to have their wards expect more from government. They envision themselves ruling a massive Department of Happiness and Fulfillment (DHF) which would be part of entitlement programs and would stamp out the vile discrimination that keeps people from happiness. Marxologists are always eager to exploit and channel any grievance against society, especially "that feeling of being thwarted and ill treated which is the auto-therapeutic attitude of the unsuccessful many."[13] The Marxologist listens to the grievance and hands the complainer a slogan. "You may be unhappy today," he adds, "but tomorrow you may become part of the Vanguard of History. Or perhaps even a dictator."

Free institutions, as it happens, are only a political framework for individuals to work out their own lives. They can guarantee no personal success or fulfillment whatsoever, much less happiness. If a rather callous man—Don, let us call him—with an IQ in the low nineties and poor hand-eye coordination, fails to become a brain surgeon or airline pilot, he has no case against democracy. If a young woman named Jacquie with a heart of gold but a face like a warthog and no dramatic talent does not realize her dream of becoming a wealthy star of stage and screen, she cannot blame Jefferson, Madison, and Adams. Instead of sitting at a keyboard all day, I would be quite pleased to play hockey on a line with Wayne Gretzky, or start at guard for the Lakers beside Earvin Johnson. If those who are hiring for these positions do not feel my gifts will get the job done, and hire someone else, I cannot scream "discrimination," or that it is "society's fault." I should add that Don, Jacquie, and myself would all have much less chance to be anything worthwhile, or even to possess the basic necessities of life, under modern neo-feudal arrangements.

These issues of fulfillment have nothing to do with the objective fact of free political institutions. They proceed from the redefinition of freedom by hierophants of the Higher Therapy, who, like Rollo May, often quarrel with or ignore the whole idea of political freedom. Religious writers do this too.

> Especially in the Western world, but hardly confined there, aspirations to freedom were very strong. But when I looked at the people I was living with as pastor—fairly affluent, well educated, somewhat knowledgeable about the Christian faith—I realized how unfree they were. They were buying expensive security systems to protect their possessions from burglary.[14]

The man with the security system may have a problem with covetousness, and may struggle with an uptight personality, but there are many senses in which he *is* free. He is not in jail, he may go where he likes, say what he likes, emigrate if he chooses, organize a political party, and so on. The people who steal from him are the ones who need lessons in morality and likely have "unfree" personalities.

Redefinitions of freedom have to do with subjective awareness, with the emotional primacy of modern culture, with false promises of Nirvana, with the notion that it is from government that all blessings flow. They also have to do with—dare one say it?—the legitimization of envy so rampant everywhere.

Envy is the unmentionable sin of New Class victorianism. Civil servants who are set for life with cost-of-living indexed pensions and every imaginable fringe benefit, are fond of lecturing on "private sector" greed, even as they demand more from the public and vote accordingly. Television anchormen, with million-dollar salaries, also elevate greed (by which they mean capitalism) above the Seven Deadly Sins. When will they take on pride, or envy, or lust?

In Western societies idea fashions come and go like shoe styles. At present, it is more important to get what you want, to *feel* free than to *be* free. And with the unqualified fulfillment of dreams held as a political right, little wonder that references to "our so-called freedoms" are taken as a badge of progressive status.

RESEARCH EXPERIMENT 1: Pose the following question: "What do you think freedom means?" to the head of the sociology or psychology department at a major university, a World War II veteran, a news anchorwoman, your Republican member of Congress, an imprisoned convict, a homosexual activist, the head of the National Council of Churches, a refugee from Bulgaria, a plumbing contractor, a wealthy female rock singer, the principal of a private school, the head of the Screen Actors Guild. Have them keep their answers short.

What were their initial reactions? Did their eyes widen? Did any become angry? How did their answers differ? Can you discern any pattern of response?

Optional: Write your findings in article form to the best of your ability and attempt to publish them. If you are a political science student, suggest this theme as a thesis topic.

RESEARCH EXPERIMENT 2: Write a one-act play in which two characters, both in the same jail cell, argue about freedom.

RESEARCH EXPERIMENT 3: On a Saturday afternoon, slip away by yourself somewhere and feel free. Maintain this feeling through Tuesday evening. If unsuccessful, repeat as many times as necessary.

CHAPTER 1, NOTES

1. John Reed was the author of *Ten Days that Shook the World*, a worshipful account of the Bolshevik Revolution. Lenin contributed a foreword. Reed is the only American buried in the Kremlin.
2. By "New Class" I mean the rough equivalent of: socialist, ideologist, redistributionist, liberal (in America), leftist, utopian, or progressive.
3. This author has also found this view to be dogmatically held and vociferously defended by some lifelong socialists of the Canadian New Democratic Party.
4. See "The Gulag vs. The Free World," James H. Dundas, *Christianity Today*, 4 October 1985, 9. The author refers to a previous news story about a Russian pastor finally released from a labor camp and allowed to emigrate to the West. Dundas refers to the "free world" but concludes: "Would Yuri's deliverance really be only an escape from one gulag to another of a different kind?"
5. Rollo May, *Freedom and Destiny* (New York: Norton, 1981), 12-13.
6. Tom Sine, *The Mustard Seed Conspiracy* (Waco, Tex.: Word Books, 1981), 54.
7. Max Weber, *The Protestant Ethic and the Spirit of Capitalism* (New York: Charles Scribner's Sons, 1958), 45.

8. Thomas Jefferson, quoted in George F. Will, *Statecraft as Soulcraft* (New York: Simon and Schuster, 1983), 71.

9. Robert Nisbet, *Twilight of Authority* (New York: Oxford University Press, 1975), 72.

10. Ronald Berman, "Feeling Free," in *On Freedom*, ed. John Howard (Greenwich: Devin-Adair, 1984), 100.

11. G. K. Chesterton, *All Is Grist* (New York: Dodd, Mead, & Co., 1932) 31.

12. Alexis de Toqueville, *Democracy in America* (New York: Doubleday, 1969), 538.

13. Joseph Schumpeter, *Capitalism, Socialism, and Democracy* (New York: Harper and Row, 1962), 6.

14. Eugene Peterson, *Traveling Light: Reflections on the Free Life* (Downers Grove, Ill.: InterVarsity Press, 1982), 11.

CHAPTER 2
WHAT FREEDOM IS

DIVIDING THE INDIVISIBLE

We have already mentioned that nobody opposes freedom in principle. Many if not all political tyrannies include it in their constitutions. But what do they and all those trendy Westerners who scoff at "our so-called freedoms" have in mind?

"Your fine talk about so-called free elections and the so-called free enterprise system is all very well," says the New Class activist, index finger stabbing the air, "but what about freedom from hunger? What do you have to say about that, mister free enterprise? Answer that one, if you will!" The bureaucratic bleachers and the United Nations burst with cheers. There is also applause from various church headquarters. The activist (who may also be a prophet) then sits down with a kind of glow, certain he has achieved a resounding philosophical and rhetorical victory that has sent the Dark Forces of Reaction into ignominious retreat. But it is all a dream. As it happens, there is a very basic answer to this kind of question.

There are any number of legitimate human aspirations which, however necessary and wonderful they may be, cannot be linked to a definition of freedom. Their absence does not necessarily indicate a condition in which freedom does not exist. At the present time my family has plenty to eat, but it is an abuse of language and a philosophic imposture to say that we are "free from hunger." Professor Leszek Kolakowski of Oxford University proposes this test for definitions of freedom: What human claims can be satisfied in concentration camps?[1]

In any sort of prison arrangement one is often well-fed, clothed, and even supplied with all sorts of therapy as well as recreational opportunities. John Hinckley, the mentally disturbed gun collector and film buff who shot Ronald Reagan, is in fact being allowed to get married while in custody. But even if he experiences marital bliss, an unlikely prospect however crazy they are about each other, he is not free to leave his loony bin, for which Mr. Reagan is doubtless thankful. Prisoners of all types often have their basic needs met but are not free in any meaningful sense. Leave the doors unlocked and they will do their best Carl Lewis imitation. Though indeed free from hunger, so strong is their preference for the real stuff—100 proof freedom—that they will go to great lengths to break out.

"Freedom from hunger" is reductionist; it makes liberty an anatomical or even zoological concept, equivalent to a full stomach and a clean cage. This same standard applies to prisoners who spend their days mining gold or stamping out license plates. Though technically "free from unemployment," when their term has expired they do not linger, but leave whether or not a job awaits them.

The list of pseudo-freedoms is endless and continually expanding: freedom from anxiety, from neurosis, from loneliness, from poverty. There is even a society promoting freedom from religion. All these have great appeal partly because they appear to follow the freedom *from* principle. When we get into the freedom *to* section, the list goes on forever. In practice, these freedoms are really considered by their advocates to be *rights* which the government must guarantee to every citizen, even if it has to make everyone a ward of the state in the process.

Behind all this lie two fallacies: (1) there is a hierarchy of freedom in which some freedoms are more important than others; (2) the notion that freedom is divisible, that some freedoms can be enhanced by limiting or eliminating others. The following is a classic statement of the idea:

> Free-enterprise economics is often defended on the basis that it promotes freedom and an open society. This idea, however, is a fallacy. It certainly increases the freedom of some, but always and inevitably at the expense of the freedom of others. Freedom is not an ever-expanding commodity. If there is going to be more real freedom of economic choice (both to produce and to consume) at the bottom end of society, then there have to be restrictions placed on the freedoms of those who can influence economic policies at the top end.[2]

There are many problems in this passage—zero-sum thinking, class analysis, and so on that will be dealt with later. There are also a number of unanswered questions, principally this: Who will do the restricting that will "have to be" done? What if people don't like the restricting? Will they be punished? Setting these aside for the moment, the strategy is clear that the author wants to restrict freedom in the name of freedom, ostensibly for the benefit for those at "the bottom." This is a very seductive line of reasoning and finds many takers, myself included at one time. But such a thing cannot be done. Freedom is indivisible.

To say that freedom is indivisible is not the same as saying there can be different grades of freedom in any given situation. It must be remembered that absolute freedom is an illusion and a slogan—unless you happen to be Robinson Crusoe. But the fact that freedom can be graded does not mean that we may not distinguish between a free society and one that is not. Practically we don't usually have to, since it is done for us by builders of walls and stringers of barbed wire.

In a free society, *individuals* are better judges of their interests than the state or any collective entity. In short, the individual is free to choose how he will live. But how can the individual pursue his interests if there is central control of economic policy? How can he make his views known if the government controls media? How can he express his political will if all parties but one are banned?

Though freedom is indivisible, it will suit our purpose here to split it up into component parts (in no particular order) for purposes of examination—an intellectual dissection, as it were. We will then put it back together again. Some of this may seem painfully obvious, but as Orwell wrote, it is a duty to restate the obvious. It may be true that part of our problem lies in the inability to learn truths that are too difficult. But, as the proverb goes, we also forget truths that are too simple. There is too much we take for granted.

FREEDOM OF MOVEMENT

This most definitely cannot pass Kolakowski's concentration camp test. It is an example of a freedom not appreciated until it is lost or taken away—both clear possibilities. Those of us who jump in our cars and drive where we please seldom think about it, but on this basic freedom much depends.

The immigrants from all over the world who populated North America were people who, as the saying goes, "voted with their feet." Denied economic opportunity or political rights or religious freedoms in their native countries, they simply left; they made conscious decisions as to where they would live and under what kind of authority they would place themselves.

Since liberty of movement is visible, and probably the purest expression of freedom, it is viciously suppressed by tyrannies. In past ages, structures like China's Great Wall were built to keep invaders out; they are now put up to keep people in, the Berlin Wall being the classic case.

Paul Goring, professor of psychology at the University of Antioquia in Medellín, Colombia, and a personal friend, finally managed to visit a relative in East Germany he had not seen for many decades. The first thing this relative told him was: "I'm a prisoner here."

Never before in history have tyrannies been so total that, given any chance to escape, people will leave everything and flee like antelope. More than a tenth of Cuba's population has departed and more would leave if they could. Cuban novelist Fernando Arrabal, now living in France, writes in "to Fidel Castro," an open letter:

> For if your battleships were to lift the blockade to which you subject your own people, the pearl of the Antilles would be converted into the island of Robinson Crusoe.[3]

Freedom of movement—free emigration if you like—cannot be allowed by tyrannies because it is the ultimate verdict on the system and the people who run it. Departure is a political statement, an act of defiance. In spite of the dangers, people still flee, often using the most ingenious of methods. A group from Mainland China, for example, set sail on a raft made of over twenty-eight thousand inflated condoms.[4] This is the century of the refugee.

For those still in the compound, there exists an elaborate system of travel restrictions and an internal passport to be carried by all citizens. Not only is movement restricted, but people are forced to live where the rulers tell them. When people are allowed to go where they please, movement is usually from country to town. Some modern tyrannies reverse this. Witness the absurd Cambodian regime goose-stepping people out of the cities into rural collectives. China banishes its free spirits to backwater farms where they can be happy and free from unemployment planting rice and distributing the night soil. The South African government limits movement and herds its subjects into bogus "homelands." Similarly, Julius Nyerere's collectivist doctrine of *Ujamaa* has uprooted millions from their traditional areas.

It can now perhaps be better understood that some freedoms cannot be eliminated to enhance others. What is left after freedom of movement is taken away? Not much.

Freedom of movement is not only the exception in today's world, it is positively endangered. Ancient Greece had its philospher-kings; the modern world has seen the rise of the philosopher-jailer: Castro, Pol Pot, Mikhail Gorbachev. The beatific vision of the latter group is a world in which the walls can finally be broken down, not because of peace or advances in human rights, but because there is no longer a place to run, no city of refuge.

An author writing in *Writer's Digest* counsels would-be novelists to avoid self-pity, which he says is a destructive emotion for a writer. He urges those feeling sorry for themselves to read *One Day in the Life of Ivan Denisovich*. This is solid advice for anyone, especially those who are told that liberty of movement is a "so-called freedom."

FREEDOM OF SPEECH

Yakov Smirnoff, a Russian emigré and comedian, offers this insight into our subject. He tells us that in America he is free to go downtown and announce to everyone: "I hate President Reagan!" for which statement he is not subjected to any criminal penalty. Not one to shortchange his homeland, he adds that in Kiev or Moscow, he can also go downtown and shout: "I hate President Reagan!" with similar freedom from prosecution. Were he to publicly express similar disapproval of, say, that barrel of laughs Andrei Gromyko, the results would be different. This is doubtless why Yakov Smirnoff, along with a host of other Russian performers, writers, poets, and artists, no longer live in their homeland.

In free societies the limitations to freedom of speech are remarkably few. There is of course no absolute freedom of speech. The classic example is that no one is free to yell "fire!" in a crowded theatre. The libel laws are the other check. One may publicly state that a provincial premier has had sexual liaisons with caribou, but not without fear of a law suit if the charge is not true. The civil rights laws in the United States forbid teachers from making disparaging remarks about the race, national origin, and religious creed of their students.

Libel laws are much stricter in Canada and England than they are in the United States; this is an example of the gradation of freedom referred to earlier. But though their restrictions on freedom of speech are different, they are questions of degree not kind. All three countries are free societies. And for the most part, for better or for worse, anything goes.

For example, the 1983 *Writers Market* includes an entry for a magazine called *Undinal Songs*, "The Only International Magazine Focusing on Necrophilia and Vampirism in Modern Literature." The editors are looking for "a personified Death or necrophilic experience that you would care to share with readers." While this example relates more to press freedom, it more or less defines the current climate of all expression. Whether one speaks out in favor of necrophilia or mounts a soapbox and renders a spirited impression of Karl Marx or Lenin, all is permitted.

However, a sidebar to this subject is that those who with great passion proclaim themselves champions of speech freedom are quick to deny it to others. Jeane Kirkpatrick, while American ambassador to the United Nations, was invited to speak at a college but was prevented from doing so by a vocal group of student "radicals." They did not want to merely disagree with the ambassador but insisted that she not be heard at all. Michael Novak, who treats his opponents with the utmost respect, has had similar experiences of local censorship. Would freedom of speech exist in a country run by such champions of fairness?

Under any conditions when political criteria are used to determine what may be said, and when government officials cannot be openly criticized, freedom of speech does not exist.

Government control of media is also inimical to free speech. The British Broadcasting Corporation (BBC) once held a broadcast monopoly in England. For a number of years, Winston Churchill was banned from the airwaves for purely political reasons. To allow him to speak was thought to "play into the hands" of "militarists" when, in fact, it was militarists in Europe that he wanted to warn the populace about. Had Churchill been able to counter the appeasement buffooneries of Neville Chamberlain, England would perhaps not have been so unprepared for Hitler's aggressive machinations. Little wonder that Orwell used the BBC as the model for his Ministry of Truth in 1984. In similar style, conservatives are notoriously unrepresented on the Canadian Broadcasting Corporation (CBC) and American Public Broadcasting System (PBS). If these networks had a monopoly, it is doubtful whether conservatives would be heard at all.

Needless to say, the Marxist totalitarian states are the worst offenders here. Even South Africa allows detractors of the regime like Desmond Tutu to travel the world denouncing apartheid. The Eastern bloc gags its dissidents or does away with them altogether, sometimes en masse. In the West, those who would change existing institutional arrangements write best-sellers and make appearances on "The Phil Donahue Show."

FREEDOM OF THE PRESS

A relative of socialist inclinations once told me, quite dogmatically, that the press in the United States was controlled by the government. This revelation, coming as it did around the Watergate period, was quite a shock. If the U.S. government controlled the press, why did it allow a continuous torrent of damaging attacks upon itself? For those who make this ridiculous charge this is a great and abiding mystery.

Similarly, I heard David Duke, a spokesman for the Ku Klux Klan, tell radio host Larry King that the American press was "controlled by Jews." The charge was delivered with such elan that it was clear the speaker believed it to be common knowledge, denied only by Zionists and their nefarious agents. In fact, the notion of a cabal of Jews controlling the media is an anti-Semitic ghost story and racist fantasy. The American press is replete with stories criticizing Israel. Mr. Duke obviously does not read *The Nation*.

Since that time, I have written for a number of national magazines and newspapers, such as the *San Diego Union*; I am happy to report that no effort has been made by the United States government to control me—or for that matter, by the government of any country. Neither have Zionist agents tampered with my copy. In any case, if they or anybody else attempted such a thing, they would have little success. I am speaking for myself here, but a thousand other writers would say the same thing.

Freedom of the press is simply freedom of speech extended to publishing. In this arrangement, writers and publishers freely express their views on all manner of subjects without consulting the higher authorities or submitting their copy for approval. There are no taboo subjects; there are no persons off limits, as a look at *Mother Jones* magazine will verify. Libel no one and you may say what you please. In a free society, the range of expression is breathtaking. From the dizzying heights of *Scientific American*, *Harper's*, *Commentary*, and *Atlantic Monthly* all the way down to the dregs: *National Enquirer*, *Playgirl*, *Screw* magazine, and the *Daily Worker*. It's all here. If freedom of the press does not exist in the United States, it exists nowhere.

Fortunately, press freedom tends to be more zealously guarded than others because of the high profile and thin skin of journalists. Even those scribes who gush over the U.N. and favor government redistribution of wealth reached for their Smith and Wessons when Amabou M'Bow of Senegal, crown prince of UNESCO, started hawking a "New World Information Order." This was one Newspeak phrase for which journalists supplied their own subtitles; the man was talking censorship and propaganda. In this New Order, only government-approved journalists would be allowed to work, and there would be restrictions on the kind of stories they could write. Anything embarrassing to a Third World dictatorship, even if true, would not be allowed. It was all portrayed, of course, as a plan that would be of great benefit to everyone, especially the Third World, and which would stamp out "information imperialism." The response of the United States was to drop out of UNESCO[5], a most wise choice, soon to be followed by Britain and hopefully others. Many journalists broke stride and applauded these moves. They understand that freedom of the press is the very lifeblood of their profession. If only they would guard all freedom—especially freedom of enterprise—with similar vigor.

The same sort of controlled arrangement M'Bow proposed for the whole world already exists in many dictatorships. The term, "Soviet journalist," is an oxymoron. Journalists in all Eastern bloc countries are really civil servants publicizing what Hemingway called, "that so malleable substitute for the Apostle's Creed—the Party line."[6] One day they are heaping abuse on Hitler's Reich; the next day, after the Nazi-Soviet Pact is signed, they are praising it as an ally and attacking the anti-Nazi efforts of the West. They are the inquisitors and hagiographers of the state religion. Of course, when there is no freedom of the press, the people are kept in ignorance and the government can do—and does—pretty much as it pleases.

Czech novelist Milan Kundera writes that in such a restricted society run by terror, no press statements at all are taken seriously, and that "it is the duty of every honest man to ignore them."[7]

I am fond of picking on the Soviets. This is entirely intentional and done without apology because they deserve it, and because New Class apologists in the West are always trying to get us to "understand" them. The trouble is, I do. But Nicaragua, too, serves as an example.

There, even under a tyrant like Somoza, there was full coverage of the guerrilla war, complete with photographs and a variety of editorial opinion. Under the Marxist Sandinistas, *La Prensa*, the only independent newspaper left in the country, is so heavily censored that it is practically impossible for it to publish. Nothing that is less than worshipful of the Sandinistas is allowed. The editors know their days are numbered.

A free press system generates reeking slag heaps of garbage. Of that there can be no doubt. But no one is forced to read it. Freedom also generates much that is of high quality and varied point of view, which we select for our mental nourishment. No such choice exists under a controlled arrangement. Whether or not journalists are doing a good job (there is currently much room for improvement), a free press is an integral part of the whole indivisible concept of liberty. It is indispensible for keeping free citizens informed. Only dictators and their apprentices want to keep it shackled. Only they call telling the truth "information imperialism."

FREEDOM OF RELIGION

In some Western nations there still exists a state church; no one, fortunately, is required to join it in order to vote, hold public office, or for any reasons other than those of their own choosing. However, the thought of requiring membership and attendance along the lines of Calvin's Geneva has probably occurred to English government officials. Indeed, there is some question whether these churches would continue to exist if it were not for state support. So poor is attendance that one wag has described Church of England ministers as "museum curators."

In all the West there is freedom *from* religion for those who desire it and freedom *to believe in* and practice religion for the vast majority of the citizenry who desire it. While this author has often heard the notion that there is no liberty of speech or press freedom in America, he has never heard the contention that there is no freedom of religion. No glib socialists or Klanspersons make the charge on the "Larry King Show." Religion is all too visible and audible: Crystal Cathedrals, glossolalia on cable television, churches in every neighborhood, Oral Roberts reporting visions of a nine-hundred-foot Jesus, and so on. Many an ideologist would be capable of such a denial, but in this case, since most consider religion harmful, they do not attempt one. Rather, they point to the proliferation of religion as a proof text that allowing freedom in this area is bad.

The United States, particularly, is a pluralistic society when it comes to religion. There are orthodox Catholics, Hasidic Jews, Mormons, and Plymouth Brethren (a Protestant sect that Garrison Keillor, who grew up in it, jokes is "so small that only we and God knew it existed"). There is the intriguing religion of Scientology, which secretly teaches that seventy-five million years ago the earth was called Teegeach and was among ninety planets ruled by Xemu. This ruler, it turns out, was deeply concerned about overpopulation, a sort of primordial Paul Erlich or Phil Donahue. So concerned, in fact, that he took beings from all his subject planets, stuffed them into ten volcanoes, and blew them to smithereens with H-bombs. However, only their bodies were destroyed; their spirits, called thetans, were frozen in alcohol for thirty-six days. During this period, Xemu planted in them the seeds of aberrant behavior.[8] Why Xemu did this is something of a mystery. Whatever one thinks of this account one is free to ignore it or believe it, as celebrities like actor John Travolta and pianist Chick Corea do.

One should also mention the Rastafarian religion, which venerates former Ethiopian emperor Haile Selassie. (Why him, one wonders?) In fact, with the proliferation of new religions—cults, if you like—one sometimes longs for a chat with an orthodox, old-fashioned atheist, the kind that is so angry at God for existing that he oraculates like Billy Sunday. But it remains clear that man is so incurably religious that, in a generally secular age, he will invent new religions. This is sad, since the old ones worked fine.

This is no place for a full discussion of church-state issues—that has already been masterfully done by Richard John Neuhaus in *The Naked Public Square*—but one must say that although the United States Congress is forbidden to es-

tablish an official state church, it is also forbidden to interfere with the free exercise of religion. Freedom of religion is
currently imperiled by government harassment.

The Amish, for example, have been periodically harassed by the Internal Revenue Service and other government agencies. They neither pay into Social Security nor accept any benefits of it. This does not go down well with bureaucrats looking at budget deficits and staff cuts. The Amish
also refuse to be innoculated against various diseases, which
has given rise to scare stories shamelessly fanned by the electronic media. These people have fled persecution in other
lands, and it is their right to live in peace and freedom here.
Nothing they do merits harassment.

Mainstream pacifists too have taken their share of
abuse. This author is not a pacifist and believes that pacifism
involves a dimension of parasitism. As public policy it is irresponsible and suicidal. But it is nonetheless the belief of
some, and a free society allows it. There have been many
nonpacifists willing to lay down their lives so that pacifists
might be free to be passive.

Christian educators in Nebraska have been jailed for
employing teachers who did not possess a state credential.
Certain pastors went to jail rather than give in to this demand. This is clear harassment and has no place in a free society.

Bob Jones University is an ultrafundamentalist school
that does not allow interracial dating, though it does admit
blacks. Practically all Christians, including leading biblical
scholars, find no support for this or for any "separation of the
races" theory. Indeed the early church was racially mixed
from the beginning and taught that humanity is one (Acts
17:26). I find the Bob Jones outlook not only unbiblical but
incredibly petty. But whether one agrees or not, is it right for
the IRS to harass this group and remove their tax exemption
because their practice is against an official perception of the
"public policy"? Even those who find the racial views of BJU

completely wrong and harmful think not—William Ball and several Supreme Court justices for instance.

Slavery was once American public policy. Would it have been right for government officials to harass those churches that opposed slavery? Christian doctrine and social activism, after all, formed the very flywheel of the anti-slavery and civil rights movements.

Hence, for true freedom of religion to exist, religion, however much we disagree with its form, must be free from arbitrary molestation by government. The exception of course is when the tenets of the religion break civic laws. Such things as human sacrifice are not allowed and, to put it mildly, interfere with the freedom of others. There are of course gray areas, but a free society with an independent judiciary is well capable of adjudicating such matters. As long as belief in, say, Xemu and Teegeach affects only the willing adherents of the faith, it should be left alone as the law stipulates.

Freedom of religion cannot flourish when this popular nostrum prevails: "The public square is off limits to religiously based values." As Richard John Neuhaus so capably points out in *The Naked Public Square*, this is a rather novel idea. What it actually represents is the state adopting secularism as official policy. Though the American state is forbidden to establish an official religion, the phrase "separation of church and state" nowhere appears in the Constitution; there is only an Establishment Clause and a Free Exercise Clause.

Religiously based values are the only kind that exist. One can no more invent a new value than one can add a new color to the spectrum. If public policy were kept immune from religious influence, there would be no laws against murder or theft. There would have been no antislavery or civil rights movement. Christian clergymen and social activists like Martin Luther King, under the "separation" dogma, would be told to go to the back of the bus and accept the status quo. Liberty, civil rights, and social justice cannot survive the death of faith or the silencing of religious activism. Free societies require the cultivation of virtue, and this is one of religion's traditional roles.

Yet, the secular separation dogma is widespread. Witness the American Civil Liberties Union, a willing advocate for all kinds of student causes but an opposer of the right of students to meet privately, under their own initiative, for Bible study on school property. They believe this constitutes an official establishment of religion, which is nonsense. The public school system of the city of New York has a special school for homosexuals and yet it is claimed this does not imply approval of homosexuality. But any public funds going to a private school, even though provided by the taxes of those very citizens, is thought to constitute a state establishment of religion. This is a clear double standard. If only the kids wanted to form a Gay Rights League or a General Jaruzelski Fan Club, then ACLU lawyers would leap to their defense. It is a blatant example of secular, antireligious bias.

Opposition to religious freedom is not the sole property of Marxist dictatorships, though they are among the worst offenders. In the USSR and Albania, anyone who deviates from Party dogma is considered mentally ill and such ones are often tossed into asylums. But Party theologians no longer predict the complete demise of religion. Over sixty years of vicious persecution and atheistic indoctrination have been unable to eliminate it. This is a cause for much rejoicing. Unfortunately, religion in most Marxist lands is now both officially tolerated and used. Religious officials are put to work justifying government tyranny, informing on their countrymen, linking Party "peace" doctrines with those of the Christian faith, and acting as tour guides to the denizens of naivete who come to see how the future works. This is how the official clergy in Marxist lands earn their check. (How I would love to see a study on the suicide rates amoung such people.) But the Marxists hold no monopoly.

Various African countries have attacked and deported Jehovah's Witnesses. Christian Armenians in Turkey were slaughtered in huge numbers. Idi Amin also persecuted Christians. To this day, Indian Hindus launch pogroms against Muslim refugees from Bangladesh. The Ayatollah Khomeini will not tolerate members of the B'hai faith. Protestants were once viciously persecuted in Colombia, and even in Quebec. Catholics in Northern Ireland have been repressed. Modern states in which people can practice the religion of their choice, without fear of death, harm, or relegation to second-class citizenship, have been all too rare.

FREEDOM OF ENTERPRISE

Authors, professors, and artists of all denominations would go to the stake to protect freedom of thought and expression; erotic poets would take to the barricades for freedom of speech. Journalists, who staunchly defend freedom of the press, have been known to go to jail rather than reveal their sources. (Apparently the public's "right to know" does not apply here.) But raise the question of free enterprise in these quarters and see what happens. It will often be vociferously denied that freedom of enterprise is any kind of human right at all.

I will deal at length on free enterprise later in the book, but a few things must be said at this point. Under the feudal system, people were required to take up the occupation of their parents or one chosen by the feudal lord. From each was taken according to his ability, to each was given according to his need. It was an occupational caste system similar to the one that still exists in India. The feudal barons, like their modern successors, found it very much to their liking; they controlled both economic and political power—a sure prescription for tyranny. Within its strict limitations, feudalism worked as long as the serfs did what they were told.

With the rise of industrial capitalism, people began to leave the feudal manors and pour into the market towns or *bourgs*. This is the origin of the word *bourgeois* (town-dweller), which is now a popular term of abuse. Socialists say of someone that he is "bourgeois" or "has a bourgeois mind" the way a feudal robber-baron might have commented that a slum-dweller was "underbred" or a British colonial official might have lamented that a native politician was of the "lower races." In current usage, "bourgeois" is a synonym for "exploitive," "unjust," or "obsolete."[9]

A bourgeois freed from the feudal plantation may have lacked security but that did not appear to matter. The act of departure meant that the rhythms and patterns of his life were no longer fixed. There were other disadvantages but the good points easily outweighed these. The intelligent, industrious bourgeois formerly conscripted for life into digging potatoes or fixing shoes could now work at whatever calling suited his skills, gifts, inclination, and the public demand. If it did not please him to work for someone else, he could start his own business, and many did. The market—simply a mirror of human needs and wants—determined his economic activity, not the whims of a feudal lord. He was, in short, a free man. And the bourgeois society formed by these former serfs, while far from perfect, raised an important bulwark against the Leviathan of state power. In the world as it exists and has always existed, power checks power. Many an aspiring tyrant has learned the hard way that free people are not easily pushed around.

While revisionist historians and New Class theologians view bourgeois society as a squalid vale of tears and a distillery of alienation, here is what Karl Marx had to say about it:

> The bourgeoisie, during its rule of scarce one hundred years, has created more massive and more colossal productive forces than have all preceding generations together. Subjection of Nature's forces to man, machinery, application of chemistry to industry and agriculture, steam-navigation, railways, electric telegraphs, clearing of whole continents for cultivation, canalization of rivers, whole populations conjured out of the ground—what earlier century had even a presentiment that such productive forces slumbered in the lap of social labor?[10]

Even Marx, the unkempt *enragé* who never worked a day in his life, was not so blind that he failed to see the successes of bourgeois capitalism while he was pointing out its shortcomings. Little wonder that toward the end of his life he claimed, "I am not a Marxist."[11] One can only speculate what he would say if he saw all that had been done in his name by his more benighted disciples.

So much for the accomplishments of bourgeois society. They are what happen when a system of natural liberty is in place, as opposed to any coercive model, even one that imagines itself benevolent. The engine of this productive system of natural liberty is freedom of enterprise—free people using their God-given talents in the field of their choice. Their limitations are remarkably few: their own gifts and energies, the rights of others, the demands of the market, the laws against fraud and coercion. Otherwise, free people create their own enterprise. As we will show later, the whole society benefits from a free system, just as the whole society is harmed by a coercive system. This system of liberty is not American, Canadian, or Belgian; it is not "based on greed"; it is not "exploitive." It is a gift of God and a fundamental human right.

A current curiosity is that secularists endeavor to show that human beings are the result of a long, impersonal process of evolution. In this view we are part of the animal kingdom; anthropology is really zoology. And yet, it is thought necessary to restrict human activity—enterprise—in a form that would be thought illegitimate with any other animal. These secularists are still acting on memories of the Judeo-Christian doctrine of the primacy of man. But even according to the zoological view, human beings have a right to free enterprise, just as a beaver has a right to build a dam.

Whatever our views on human origins, it is idle to talk of a free society without freedom of enterprise. People deprived of this are not true citizens at all, or even, as has been mentioned, true human beings; they are only The Masses or The Workers, an aggregation of electro-chemical humanoids going about their robot functions at the behest of Wise Planners. The alienation and greed that surges from this system dwarfs anything capitalism ever produced.

Many a turgid tome has been penned to show the benefits of a centrally planned economy as opposed to a free one. Those hostile to freedom of enterprise cite various reasons for their stance, but, as Milton Friedman noted: "underlying most arguments against the free market is a lack of belief in freedom itself."[12] We will discuss this problem in the section on ideology. The current contempt for free enterprise "bourgeois" society reveals not only a lack of belief in freedom but a latent hatred for it. This is a most unhealthy situation.

FREEDOM OF ASSOCIATION

In 1979 a member of the Communist party USA spoke in San Diego. He urged his listeners to give up their color television sets and contribute to The Cause, the never-ending class struggle. "If there is an ounce of hatred in you," he said, "then give." The media covered the meeting and no one interfered. There were no arrests made because nothing was illegal.

Indeed, the church to which I belong (Presbyterian Church USA) once contributed to the legal defense fund of Angela Davis, a presidential candidate of the American Communist party. Though outrageous (but not unusual) conduct for a Christian church, there was nothing illegal about this. Nobody pressed charges.

In a society where freedom of association exists, one may join any political party, even one like CPUSA that advocates the violent overthrow of that very society and its replacement with a Marxist dictatorship. Only when the tactical divisions of such parties—the Weather Underground and Symbionese Liberation Army, for instance—begin the actual demolition with bullets and dynamite do the police, rightly, intervene. Otherwise, it's all legal, at least in North America: from the satirical Rhinocerous party to the

Progressive Conservatives; the New Democratic party; the GOP; the Social Credit party; the Socialist Workers party; the Bull Moose party (now defunct); the National Socialist White People's party; Communist party USA; and a host of others in a wide variety of ideological colors—Greens, Reds, Blacks, Grays, and assorted shades of Pink. Take your pick; join whom you will. This is your right in a society where freedom of association exists.

Dictatorships, on the other hand, monopolize political power and often ban all parties but one and all unions except those subservient to the government. Even to associate with the opposition can bring penalties, as is the case in the Soviet Union. Mexico has been ruled by one party for nearly sixty years. It allows opposition groups but blatantly rigs the elections. "Vote early, vote often," is how one Mexican writer put it. Needless to say, Mexico has no monopoly on such things.

Free association in a political sense is meaningless without free elections, which means: absence of fraud, absence of coercion, a meaningful choice of alternatives for the voter, and, where applicable, international supervision of the proceedings. A mechanism for the peaceful transfer of power is also essential. These are all too rare in today's world. Fortunately in Western societies one may still choose one's own friends, communities, and political parties without fear of reprisal. When this right of free association and political activity has been surrended "temporarily" in the interest of "building a new society," it has seldom, if ever, been recovered. Prudence says it must never be surrendered at all.

THE REAL THING: FREEDOM IS ONE

Much more could be said about each of these categories and the way they are worked out in society. These are the basic principles of freedom as it exists in history and in the real world. Though they can be examined individually, they are ultimately indivisible and interdependent. Freedom is one. It is entirely legitimate though not in vogue to speak of free societies and free people. In the West, it is our way of life.

The ideologist, a species we shall soon study, refers to what he perceives as a superior freedom to be achieved in some future society. Whatever this perfected form of freedom is, we are told it will be much, much better than these "bourgeois" or "formal" freedoms we have been discussing. But bourgeois freedoms are the only kind that currently exist.

Human beings in a state of freedom produce both good and evil. Freedom does not mean perfection—far from it. In fact, it usually includes a lot of untidiness. But none of the foibles that exist under freedom are exorcised by taking freedom away; rather, they are often magnified. Witness the social upheavals and power struggles in socialist dictatorships. Athletes from socialist countries are no less competitive than those from democratic ones, criminals no less vicious. There have been soccer riots in Peking and Moscow as well as Liverpool and Rome. Human nature is the same in Sofia, Bulgaria, and Chicoutimi, Quebec.

Freedom is simply the natural system of liberty in which human beings work out their own destiny. It has wound down through history primarily through the Judeo-Christian tradition, along with a few other tributaries. The headwaters, as Jefferson suggested, are found in the Creator himself. A lucid but much neglected French thinker says likewise:

> God has given to men all that is necessary for them to accomplish their destinies. He has provided a social form as well as a human form. And these social organs of persons are so constituted that they will develop themselves in the clean air of liberty. . . . And now that legislators and do-gooders have so futilely inflicted so many systems upon society, may they finally end where they should have begun: May they reject all systems and try liberty; for liberty is an acknowledgement of faith in God and His works. [13]

This freedom is heady stuff, also risky and untidy. People both die for it and show an aversion to it. There is a marvelous passage in *Don Quixote* in which the brave knight and Sancho liberate a group of galley slaves.[14] But instead of showering El Quixote with gratitude, the slaves proceed to pelt him and Sancho with stones. Miguel de Cervantes knew that some people prefer freedom from unemployment to the genuine article. Thus, it is with the same sense of perplexity and sadness of the Knight of the Woeful Countenance that we turn to the study of the ideologist.

RESEARCH EXPERIMENT 1: Trace your family ancestry. Did freedom of movement play any role in it? If so, what might you be today if it had not?

RESEARCH EXPERIMENT 2: Set aside a summer and tour Canada. Bring along a motor-driven Nikon F3 and a large supply of film. Wander about taking photographs and chatting with the natives. Record how many times you are (1) told where to go by government officials, (2) prevented by same from entering an area, (3) have your equipment confiscated, (4) are deported. The next summer, repeat the experiment in Bulgaria and Albania. Interview people who have moved there from the West. Publish your findings.

RESEARCH EXPERIMENT 3: 1) Gather together all your friends who are deeply concerned about the nuclear arms race, but keep the number under five hundred. Hold a peaceful demonstration outside a nuclear power plant.

2) In a major American or Western European city, hold a peaceful demonstration protesting American missiles, the American Strategic Defense Initiative, and the French *Force de Frappe*.

3) Repeat steps 1 and 2 at suitable sites in Czechoslovakia and Leningrad, this time concentrating on the Soviet role in the nuclear arms race and the Soviet Strategic Defense Initiative. Include at least seventy-five Soviet citizens (with proper racial and gender balance, and equal representation from the various republics like Latvia) who are deeply concerned about the threat of nuclear war. If any in your group believe the Soviet Union should unilaterally disarm, have them say so. Invite local nuclear physicists to give their views on nuclear winter. If possible, distribute copies of *Time* and *Rolling Stone* magazine.

4) In what subtle ways did the television coverage of your protests differ in East and West? How many of your group want to do it again? Have your views on freedom of speech changed? If so, why?

RESEARCH EXPERIMENT 4: 1) Learn Spanish (or consult someone who does) and subscribe to *Barricadas*, the official Sandinista newspaper of Nicaragua.

2) Cut out the following: an editorial demanding the resignation of junta members for incompetence; any cartoon making fun of Comandante Daniel Ortega or his brother Umberto; an editorial against nepotism; a thoughtful essay on the dangers of alignment with Havana and Moscow; an opinion piece advocating dialogue with the *contras*; a letter to the editor by a poor campesino complaining of the $3500 spent on designer glasses by Daniel Ortega on his trip to New York; a denunciation of the invasion of Afghanistan; an investigative report on the social and psychological effects of food rationing and the block system of surveillance; a positive profile of Archbishop Obando y Bravo; a series of debates about the benefits of Marxism-Leninism; poetry by Ruben Dario; a report on the recent itinerary of the Pope; guest editorials by heads of opposition parties; any political advertisement by an opposition party; an investigative report on prison conditions, complete with photos and interviews; an opinion survey of people who have left the country and their reasons for so doing; a gossip article on Tomas Borge's mansion and Mercedes-Benz.

3) Send these articles, or any on similar themes, to me in care of the publisher.

RESEARCH EXPERIMENT 5: Go over the past two weeks (or more) of your life. Which activities depend on the freedoms mentioned in the previous chapters? Imagine life without them. Meditate on this for half an hour.

RESEARCH EXPERIMENT 6: Interview former U.S. ambassador to the U.N., Andrew Young. Ask if he still believes there are "thousands of political prisoners in the United States." If he does, select thirty specific cases and study them, using the Freedom of Information Act. Find out how many are jailed not for any acts of violence, but for simple membership in a party or for their beliefs. Inform the ACLU of all violations.

RESEARCH EXPERIMENT 7: Accompany a peace group from a church organization on a good will tour to Cuba. Request an audience with Fidel Castro. Ask if he is going to run in the upcoming elections. How tough is the opposition? Can he hold them off? What do the polls say? If possible, interview candidates from the other parties.

CHAPTER 2, NOTES
1. Leszek Kolakowski, "Beyond Empiricism," in *On Freedom*, John Howard, ed. (Greenwich: Devin-Adair, 1984), 29.
2. Andrew Kirk, *The Good News of the Kingdom Coming* (Downers Grove, Ill.: InterVarsity Press, 1984), 77.
3. Fernando Arrabal, "To Fidel Castro," *Harpers*, April 1985, 15-17.
4. *National Review*, 15 November 1985, 17.

5. There were other reasons for American withdrawal, all of them legitimate. Among them was the fact that nearly 75 percent of the UNESCO budget, most of which comes from the USA and the West, is spent at its Paris headquarters. This gives new meaning to the term "waste."

6. Ernest Hemingway, *For Whom the Bell Tolls* (New York: Charles Scribner's, Sons, 1940), 180.

7. Milan Kundera, *The Unbearable Lightness of Being* (New York: Harper Colophon, 1984), 180.

8. See "Scientologists Angry at Baring of Secrets," *San Diego Union*, 6 November 1985.

9. See Sharon Gallagher's review of *Places in the Heart* in *Eternity*, January 1985, 45. Gallagher, a Christian writer, comments that the heroine of the film struggles "against a power structure conspiring to keep her down." And yet, at the same time, she lived in a "safe, bourgeois world."

10. Karl Marx and Frederick Engels, *The Communist Manifesto* (New York: International Publishers, 1948), 13-14.

11. See Thomas Sowell, *Marxism: Philosophy and Economics* (New York: Morrow, 1985), 189.

12. Milton Friedman, *Capitalism and Freedom* (Chicago: University of Chicago Press, 1962), 15.

13. Frederic Bastiat, *The Law* (Irvington-on-Hudson: The Foundation for Economic Education, 1979), 75.

14. Miguel de Cervantes Saavedra, *Aventuras de Don Quijote de la Mancha*, adaptacion de Joaquín Aguirre Bellver (Madrid: Ediciones EDAF, 1972), 30-34.

PART

2

IDEOLOGY:
A THREAT TO FREEDOM

The conjunction of dreaming and ruling generates tyranny.
Michael Oakeshott

CHAPTER 3
A BRIEF STUDY OF IDEOLOGY

FREEDOM AS FACADE, FREEDOM AS EVIL

There is a rhythm and flow to the study of freedom. Its premises are simple and can be easily grasped and appreciated by everyone. It is more a question of reminding than of teaching. The study of ideology, however, is a messy business indeed. Nothing in it is ever what it seems. Any study of freedom that ignores it is negligent and becomes mere cheerleading. Ideology, in fact, may just be the spirit of the age.

Though the freedom discussed in the last chapter is a gift of God and part of the universal human rights of man, it has run into many obstacles on the way to full deployment. If there is any sense in which the word *progress* may have a legitimate use, it is in the sense that human beings have progressed as they have moved toward freedom and away from tyranny. This has taken a long time and involved much blood, sweat, and tears.

Right about the time when the British abolished the slave trade, when Abraham Lincoln proclaimed emancipation, when universal suffrage was being cultivated, when empires were breaking up into free and independent states, when a free market was providing abundance of food and material goods as never before, when many philanthropic and missionary organizations were sending people all over the globe, when medical science was making great strides—when it seemed for the first time that life on this earth could be something other than poor, nasty, brutish, and short—at this very time ideological ideas began their counteroffensive. This is one of the great ironies of history.

The term *ideology* in present usage can mean just about any doctrine at all, or even a philosophy or world view. But this is far too general and ultimately a confusing vulgarization. If everyone and every idea is ideological, then nothing is.

The word *ideology* was first used as *idéologie* during the French Revolution and is intrinsically bound up with the idea of revolution and the "structural" change of society.[1] Destutt de Tracy penned five volumes (1801-1815) titled *Les Éléments d'idéologie* in which the revolutionary ethos is expounded. This is a matter of history and etymology. The term was meant to be scientific, but ideology bears all the marks of a secular religion and probably gained rapid acceptance because it filled a void for those who had discarded Christianity.

Ideology is a dogma of structural or systemic evil. It holds that free Western nations are not truly free, and that they alienate people, whether they know it or not. Therefore the present structures, not individuals, need to change in order for society to be redeemed. Ideology holds out a promise of social redemption, which is often weak on the practical side. Much stronger is ideological demonology; the ideologist has a theory why people oppose him. These tenets and others will be expanded and examined in the following study.

Among other things, ideology is the heresy of the eyes. Its great discovery is that, contrary to all appearances and to the historical record, the free societies of Western Europe and North America are the most systematically oppressive despotisms of all time. This is held to be true internally and externally. The key word again is *system*. Freedom, in the sense we have been using, is considered by ideologists not only an illusion but a massive swindle to enslave. It is the ideologist who speaks of "freedom" in the same tone of voice (and usually with the same facial expression) he would use if he discovered a hair in his soup. It is the ideologist who writes scornfully of our "so-called freedoms." In this view, history is a chronicle of oppression which continues into the present except that the current Malevolent Powers, being clever, have disguised the oppression with a *facade of freedom*. This study will refer to the ideologist as roughly equivalent to the utopian, the progressive, the New Class, the radical feminist, the socialist, and all varieties of Marxists.

These types of people will not accept the designation "ideologist." Neither did Karl Marx, who applied the term to his enemies. (This refusal will not, however, hinder this study.) They will quickly retort that the conservative is merely espousing "another ideology." But the conservative does not want to restructure society; he is wary of schemes for social redemption and rejects the notion that he is alienated. He does not shun the past but values it as a source of wisdom. Hence conservatism is really the absence or even the negation of ideology, though not of principle. Russell Kirk comments:

> Conservatism, I repeat, is not an ideology. It does not breed fanatics. It does not try to excite the enthusiasm of a secular religion. If you want men who will sacrifice their past and present and future to a set of abstract ideas, you must go to Communism, or Fascism, or Benthamism. But if you want men who seek, reasonably and prudently, to reconcile the best in the wisdom of our ancestors with the change which is essential to a vigorous civil social existence, then you will do well to turn to conservative principles. [2]

Ideologists tell us we are all slaves to alien powers of patriarchy, capitalism, consumerism, individualism, and other exotic forces not perceptible to those lacking the special insight of the ideologist himself. Or, in the case of some ethnic minorities, homosexuals, or animal-rights crusaders, the alien power is simply "society" in its entirety. Ideologists are brilliantly creative at discovering new alien powers that oppress us. But while the alarm on the ideologist's oppression detector is continually beeping, most people see only the imperfect but acceptable state of things. Thus, ideology is a peddler of secrets; it is a new, social gnosticism that has created much confusion, not to mention guilt and fear.

Since it has also created a great mess in the intellectual world, the unraveling of ideology is no easy task and cannot be accomplished in a hurry—but there can be no understanding of the modern world without such an inquiry. Few have been made, fewer still have been given the circulation they deserve.[3]

Since ideology is shrouded in the smog of abstraction, it will serve our purpose to find some analogies. These unfortunately are scarce, but there are some to be found in literature. Voltaire's durable *Candide ou L'optimisme* will serve us well as we search for images.

THE LEGIONS OF EDIDNAC

In Voltaire's tale, the wonderful Doctor Pangloss assures the young Candide that he lives in the best of all possible worlds. But then, to put it mildly, everything proceeds to go wrong.

Many people today could be called Edidnac—Candide in reverse. They are told by ideological pundits, gurus, and *savants* that everything is bad, that doom is upon us, that they are oppressed (or "unconsciously enmeshed") by many devious forces and structures, or that their very lifestyle and eating habits are the cause of the hunger and oppression of others. For two quick examples:

> As a result of our lifestyles, we are a primary cause of poverty today.[4]

> By its silence, this generation of college students helps condemn thirty-five thousand children to die of starvation each year. . . .[5]

It is an awful picture indeed, frequently worse than anything they have ever heard. They writhe and tremble, sinners in the hands of an angry pacifist. And yet, when they look around, they seem to be living in the best of all possible worlds.

Slavery has been abolished, no group is prohibited from voting; people are generally clean and healthy and live longer than ever before; the poverty line is a thousand dollars above the median income in the Soviet Union; stores are full of food; there is universal education and immunization; the transfer of power is orderly; immigrants still line up at the gates, or even crash them. In comparison with the rest of the world as it actually exists and has existed through much of history, things look very good indeed. Yet the ideologist sees only gloom, repression, and structures of domination. This is the source of much confusion to Edidnac, to say the least. He looks around and rubs his eyes but he just can't explain it, and neither can the modern equivalents of Dr. Pangloss.

Pure ideology differs greatly from the Judeo-Christian tradition that locates sin in the human will; ideologists disdain such ideas and cite evil "structures," "institutions," and "systems" as the problem. Sin is political, not personal. Get the structure right, so the argument goes, and all will be well with individuals. Whether acknowledged or not, the view includes the perfectibility of man, as Anthony Burgess comments:

> There are two forces in Western society: one which believes that man was born in original sin and is capable of performing the most terrible enormities: the other which sees man as perfectible—that it is only a matter of putting the environment right. I do not believe man is perfectible.[6]

Ideology is the discovery that we are all oppressed by evil structures, and that the duty of life is to discover what they are—generally by paying close attention to the dictums of ideologists—and then, in obedience to the superior wisdom, dedicating our lives to social liberation. The ideologist has structures that he thinks will change people for the better, as Burgess explained.

Kenneth Minogue has commented that ideology, among other things, is a footnote to Marx in the same sense that theology is a footnote to the Bible, psychology a footnote to Frèud, or philosophy is a footnote to Plato. This is a most helpful analysis. Indeed, one of the main intellectual battlefields of this century has been the "structural" question of a free/democratic society versus a collective/coercive one. At one time the upper echelons of Western Society fairly jostled with ideologists, all bursting with enthusiasm for Lenin and Stalin whose alterations of the societal structures were supposed to create a "new socialist man." The abolition of the free market was supposed to accomplish the de facto abolition of the profit motive. This, like other Marxist prophecies, failed to be fulfilled.

Just how pervasive the enthusiasm for new structures was may be seen in the comments of *Life* magazine (hardly a highbrow publication) about Stalin, the most active restructerer in history. *Life* saw him as "a combination of Tom Paine, Horace Mann, Henry Kaiser and Jim Farley, rolled together with Clifton Fadiman, George Washington, Henry Wallace, and Paul Bunyan."[7] Squads of eager pilgrims journeyed to Moscow to see how the future, under the aegis of this Great Restructurer, was working. They applauded the alteration of societal structures however many lives had to be axed by this political Paul Bunyan.[8] In fact, whole regions were deforested of their human populations. Today, only the most hard-core apologists dare to mention the once-vaunted "new socialist man" the new structures were supposed to create. He turns out to be more or less a cowering twentieth-century serf with an electronic calculator and, if he is lucky and well-connected, a television set. The contention of ideologists that people in the USSR are "people just like us" is an admission that the new, coercive structures have failed.

Another irony of special interest to Christians is the fact that, whatever may have been its consequences in the past, the "structural" analysis along with the notion that Western society is oppressive has been picked up by theologians and religious social activists. Ideology may at one time have been the "cuckoo in philosophy's nest," as Minogue also describes it; doubtless to a great degree it still is. But today some of the most pristine and vocal ideologists may be found in religious circles.

A popular writer urges "Kingdom Christians" to "dismantle the *structures* of oppression in our own nation and abroad."[9] Another exhorts the church to oppose "the dehumanizing tendencies inherent in social institutions."[10] An English author puts it this way:

> A sizeable shift in emphasis has taken place in Christian teaching and preaching from concern about individual salvation and personal integrity to concern about the dehumanizing effects of *structures*.[11]

Here are more American versions; the first cites with approval a theologian who:

> Characterizes organizational *structures* of any kind that do violence to persons as "structural evil." Certainly our task as Christians in the eighties and nineties cannot be limited to fighting personal evil.[12]

> What Pinnock's new mentors call "democratic capitalism" is in my view profoundly undemocratic and *oppressive* of the poor.[13]

Christian social action, we are told by another, "tries to reshape the *structures of society*," based on what the author believes is the biblical idea of justice. The Deity too is conscripted, "God wills *structural mechanisms* which tend to reduce the extremes of wealth and poverty—both among the people of God and society at large"[14] (italics added on above quotes). Just what these new structural mechanisms which the ideologist believes can be created would look like is something of a mystery. But there are clues about the underlying principles, if not the exact details.

Whatever they might look like, they are certainly not *voluntary* structures. Biblical examples of coercive structures cited by religious ideologists are usually the sabbatical release of debts and the Jubilee year, both found in the Old Testament. Much can be said about Old Testament practices as divine endorsements of modern collectivism. In fact they are nothing of the kind.[15] But the keynote here is that the religious ideologist finds in them a proof text against voluntary economic arrangements, even against voluntary charity. All ideologists despise voluntary (free) societal "mechanisms." Though the ideologist does not state it plainly, he believes that people must be forced into what he perceives as the correct behavior. And whatever correct behavior is, it does not involve freedom of choice. If people persist in producing and buying what they don't need, and don't give enough—and they obviously aren't, the ideologist says, for there is still hunger in the world—then their money should be taken by force and redistributed. The word "redistribution" is a staple of ideological discourse. Just who would continue to produce wealth, who would confiscate it (and how), and who would redistribute it "fairly" is less clear.

The sabbatical release and the Jubilee do provide some general principles to follow, and in fact have been cited as proofs of biblical support for private property.[16] They certainly teach that the needy must be cared for, which free societies have done imperfectly, to be sure, but better than anyone else. But the ideologist uses these passages for what they are *not*—in his view they are not voluntary and therein lies their appeal.

> Neither the sabbatical release of debts nor the Jubilee is a private arrangement of charity that *individuals are free to practice or ignore*"[17] (italics added).

The absence of voluntarism is the feature the religious ideologist finds attractive; he drafts God and the Bible in his argument against freedom. This is a daunting task because God did not make creation coercive. The rigidly secular ideologist is spared such extremes; his afflatus for social and political coercion is the natural outworking of his metaphysical vacuum. He does not believe in any kind of invisible hand, and so must provide a visible one.

The extent to which this is taken may be seen in the suggestions for punishment if nonvoluntary "structural mechanisms" are not adopted. For example, a popular writer holds that if any nation would not agree to United Nations guidelines and "postponed hard political decisions on necessary agricultural reform and population control,"[18] they should be denied food by the United States and Canada.

Since the punitive action against countries that are merely slow in implementing these structural mechanisms is to let them go hungry (presumably they would not be allowed to starve), one wonders what punitive action should be taken if these countries are not only slow in implementing these structural mechanisms but *defy* them because they are counterproductive, which they surely are. While this is certainly a grotesque strategy, religious ideologists indulge other extremes that must be mentioned.

The secular ideologists of the past generation thought that once their centralized structures had been implemented, and once brilliant and compassionate people like themselves wielded power, no further systemic change would be necessary and things would generally be fine. "Structures" would then lose all importance. In fact Marx, in what is surely his most fatuous statement, thought that the very state itself would "wither away."[19] Contrast this with the perspective of one religious ideologist who believes that after his dreams (his word) have been achieved, "societal institutions would still need restructuring."[20] A more depressing and pessimistic prospect could hardly be imagined. One wonders when the restructuring will end, if ever. It all seems like the religious ideologists' version of Trotsky's permanent revolution. No mainstream ideologist of which I am aware has ever taken things so far.

I once had to contact the editor of a radical Christian magazine to ask about some data they had published about the Salvation Army, whose philanthropic efforts were, in their view, tainted by the fact that business leaders sat on the Army's board of directors. This editor, too, had strong opinions about sinful structures; in the course of our conversation, he told me quite firmly that, "our whole society is designed to keep people poor." In other words, the present oppressive structural mechanisms in America were not in any sense accidental; they were deliberately designed that way.

This is an astonishing statement about a society that from its very inception has been a magnet to immigrants from all over the globe who were eager to leave oppressive societies and improve themselves under free arrangements. In fact, immigration was heaviest when the economy was the most free and when so-called robber barons held sway. Are these myriads of immigrants so stupid that they would seek out an order "designed to keep people poor"? Even animals flee cages and sprint for the open spaces. But it is typical that the ideologist detects oppression where the immigrant does not. The ideologist's instrument panel flashes red, the immigrant's green. Let us put this charge in perspective.

In designing American institutions, the framers of the Constitution very nearly had a clean slate on which to create a new society. Few others, if any, in history had enjoyed a similar situation. The ideologist would have us imagine something like the following:

Scene: The Constitutional Convention with all the framers present.

Washington: As president of this constitutional convention, I raise this all-important question: What kind of society do we want to establish? Any ideas, Ben? You are the senior member.

Franklin: Yes, let's design a society that will make people poor and keep them that way.
[Spontaneous cheers and much pounding of desks.]

Madison: Hear hear! By all means. Now why didn't I think of that? This is what a society should do above all else. Brilliant idea, Ben.
[Sustained applause, shouts of agreement from the others.]

Washington: Fine. We are all agreed that the aim of our society is to keep people poor.

Others: [in unison] Right.

Washington: But now the tough question arises: How can we best accomplish this? After all, we can't be content with theory. Any input here? Feel free to speak.

Hamilton: Why don't we do this. In order to hide our oppressive society, let's establish all kinds of personal freedoms and set up a limited government whose main purpose will be to guard those freedoms. That should keep the shiftless little swines poor all right.

Washington: Now why couldn't I have said that? I think he's got it. It's so simple. We just make economic activity a matter of personal initiative, thereby insuring that the stupid and lazy common people will never better themselves. And it will be all their fault. It's brilliant.

Jefferson: If we reestablished feudalism, of course, there is simply no way we can keep people poor. Why, they'd all grow rich, the scoundrels! We simply can't permit that to happen. I too vote for economic freedom as a way to make and keep people poor. And we should also let them practice religion, so they will always be dreaming of the afterlife and will never improve their condition.

Washington: Good point. Everyone agreed?

Others: Aye!

Washington: Opposed?
[silence]

Washington: Good. Now, let us repeat together this resolution.

All: [solemnly] We resolve, then, that the purpose of American society shall be to make and keep people poor, and that free enterprise democracy is the best way to accomplish this.

When pressed, those who impute malign motives to promoters of freedom would of course disavow such open scheming. Their scenario would be rather different. They would tell us that American society was only "subliminally" or "unconsciously" designed to keep people poor. More about this later.

Since ideology is also the social equivalent of morbid introspection, it should not be surprising that some religious people should become ideologists. Some branches of the Christian church, notably the Anabaptists of the Arminian tradition, are particularly susceptible to morbid introspection on a personal level. As the outlook of their respective churches grows less concerned with personal salvation, less "other-worldly," and becomes more involved with social issues and public policy, it is to be expected that the same morbid introspection will be applied to all of society. But even given this head start into ideology, the lengths to which it is taken by some religious people are truly astonishing, capable at times of surprising even the most militant secularist.

IDEOLOGY, SCIENCE, AND THE ACADEMY

Though a form of social analysis, ideology is most definitely not science. Science is occupied with the empirical, with hard evidence, with the disinterested pursuit of truth, not with the discovery of secret forms of oppression. Ideology is too preoccupied with dogma and too aloof from evidence to qualify as science. Indeed, as exemplified by writers like Marcuse,[21] the very basis of ideology is the deliberate ignoring of evidence. The relation of the ideologist to the scientific and academic community is decidedly ambivalent, though the ideologist may be an academic or scientist himself. What the ideologist wants from science and the academy is respectability, visibility, and perhaps a vocabulary. Office space and a generous grant or two are certainly not out of the question and are frequently forthcoming. The social sciences are a favorite hunting ground of ideologists.

This being so, it should be mentioned that these disciplines are not like hard sciences such as chemistry and physics. By the strictest of standards sociology and psychology are scarcely sciences at all. In fact, in the hands of ideologists they have become a respectable form of gnosticism, a discovery of secret forces in society, of statistical suffering which then become the justification for a political program.

Western societies, particularly the United States, do not elect many ideologists. This electoral flouting of her views makes the ideologist angry. Not only does the man in the street fail to see oppression on every hand, but he perversely fails to vote "correctly"—that is, for the "progressive" approved candidates. This anger is channeled into new discoveries of hidden forces that make people vote certain ways.

For a quick example, the 1984 Republican landslide is glibly attributed to the fact that Reagan is telegenic. People were not voting for his policies we are told by millionaire ideologists holding microphones and reading off teleprompters. They were not exercising their informed choice; they were charmed out of their vote by the smoothness of Ronnie the Matinee Idol. But this is nonsense. The Nixon landslide of 1972 was every bit as decisive. A less telegenic politician than Richard Nixon has never existed, with the possible exception of Joe Clark in Canada. But the ideologist can never accept the simple explanation that the vast majority of the populace (Walter Mondale barely carried his home state) do not care for ideological candidates, nor for ideology.

Many a sociological study is pure metaphysics and pontification wrapped in pseudoscientific jargon and sequined with statistics. Such studies easily become a proof text for a political agenda. In this way social science becomes political science. Robert Nisbet affirms, "It is the national state and its centralized power that is the be-all and end-all in the minds of the vast majority of social scientists in our time."[22]

P.T. Bauer sees true social science as occupied with kinship, local community, and voluntary association. But under present conditions "social scientists engender problems by discerning, announcing, and emphasizing discrepancies between their assumed norms and reality."[23]

For example, some social scientists claim that present free institutional arrangements discriminate against certain groups in society—blacks, Hispanics, women, and so on. The discovery made and given scientific approval, special status and preferential treatment for the group is advocated. In liberal societies with elected officials and no aristocratic class, the best way to get special treatment is to gain accredited victim status. The ideologist in academia develops and defines this status.

Blacks in the United States were once denied the vote. This was an arrangement that did indeed require change. Now that it has been made, it is difficult to see how universal suffrage and the rules of a free, democratic society discriminate against any particular group. Do the rules of the National Basketball Association discriminate against the short? Do the rules of horse racing discriminate against the heavy and the tall? Does the fact that nearly 100 percent of all people executed for murder in the United States are male prove that the American legal system discriminates against men?

The possibilities for a nimble ideologist operating under the mantle of social science are promising indeed. He spills out his statistics like bones or chicken entrails and gazes on them. The trouble is, his structural explanation of evil gives him a kind of retinitus pigmentosa, a narrow range of vision. There are other common breeds of ideological fungus which also affect the retina and the intellect. The reading of the statistical bones usually comes out this way: Present arrangements in Western democracies are bad and discriminatory; slick free-enterprise politicians can con the populace into votes, therefore democracy is illusory, manipulative, or not working; new structural mechanisms must be put in place.

Ideology is not science; in fact, it is much closer to magic in its methods and posture. Even as sober an analyst as

Kenneth Minogue has described it as such, and not just because of statistical voodoo. He also cites the incantory nature of ideological prose and has compared ideological doomsaying to curses.[24] Although the ideologist would repudiate the charge of magic, he sometimes distances himself from science and the academy all by himself.

Part of the reason for this is that all the sciences are now considered less exact than they once were. Scientists are no longer accepted simply because they are scientists.[25] But the ideologist who decides to chuck science has other good reasons.

Since his concern and duty is to criticize all of society (or even the world) and change all its basic institutions (even if a majority of the people do not want them changed), those who are not so occupied must also be criticized. The disinterested academic or scientist thus becomes to the ideologist a mere trafficker in trivia—a fact-grubber, a bookworm, the intellectual equivalent of someone scouring a condemned building site for butts and beer cans.

The worst possible scenario is to have the ideologist not only in power and actively restructuring society, but tampering with science as well. At Stalin's behest, Trofim Lysenko announced that genetics was determined by environment. Computer technology was declared a "bourgeois science," though this has been abandoned for obvious reasons. Similarly, Nazi-Aryan theories of "Jewish science" had to be banished for pragmatic considerations when Hitler sought to build an atomic bomb. Aryan theories of biological superiority were dealt a major blow by the exploits of Jesse Owens.

As headmaster of the Academy, the ideologist is at his creative best. He changes psychiatry—and even medicine—into a means for healing dissidents of their views. He orders that history be rewritten to give himself the Starring Role. In Marxist lands, he simplifies the curriculum of philosophy departments: only one philosophy is allowed—his.

Ideology is indeed a form of social analysis, but its method is not scientific. It does not examine historical and empirical evidence and conclude from the data that Western societies are oppressive; rather, it begins with the notion that they are oppressive and tries to make the evidence fit this dogma. It is more accurately a metaphysic, not science. Yet ideology uses science for its own ends. If the ideologist can make his case simply by saying, "I'm a scientist," he will generally do so.

In some cases ideology is a vocal opponent of the academy and of science. When it can mold science and scholarship in its own image, disaster is sure to result. A great deal of the history of this century is a casualty report on the restructuring efforts of ideologists.

To sum up, what is ideology? Many things, but principally this: It is a form of social analysis that discovers that Western societies are oppressive and alienate people, that maligns "structures" like the open market, a democratic polity, and in extreme cases even the family as the cause of this oppression, and advocates that the business of life is liberation through structural change—usually adding new coercive structures. Ideology currently finds some of its most eager acolytes in the religious community. Peruvian novelist Mario Vargas Llosa, a most perceptive writer, provides an insight into how their minds work:

> 'He confuses reality and illusion, he has no idea where the one ends and the other begins,' he said. 'It may be that he recounts those things in all sincerity and believes every word. It doesn't matter. Because he doesn't see them with his eyes but through the filter of his ideas, his beliefs. . . . It's quite possible that to him a street fight among ruffians in Barcelona or a raid on smugglers by the police in Marseilles is a battle waged by the oppressed against the oppressors in the war to shatter the chains binding humanity.'[26]

This discovery of structural oppression everywhere cannot exist in a vacuum. It has certain logical, verbal, temperamental, and procedural consequences, which will now be explored.

CHAPTER 3, NOTES

1. For the etymology and origin of ideology see Kenneth Minogue, *Alien Powers: The Pure Theory of Ideology* (New York: St. Martins, 1985), 1-7. Also Russell Kirk, "The Unnatural History of Giant Ideology," *Chronicles of Culture*, April 1986, 18-21.

2. Russell Kirk, *Prospects for Conservatives* (Chicago: Henry Regnery Co., 1956) 6.

3. This study is indebted to works by Kenneth Minogue and Tom Wolfe, especially the former. Readers who wish to imbibe deeper on this subject are referred thereto.

4. Tom Sine, *The Mustard Seed Conspiracy* (Waco, Tex.: Word Books, 1981), 26. The author also attempts to show how buying franchise hamburgers causes malnutrition in Haiti (p. 28).

5. Ronald J. Sider, "Silent Condemnation," letter to the editor of *HIS* magazine, December 1984.

6. Interview with Anthony Burgess, *MacLean's*, 28 October 1985. Quoted in *Eternity*, "Just for the Record," January 1986, 70.

7. Quoted by R. Emmett Tyrell, Jr. in "Sickle Cell Amnesia," *The American Spectator*, December 1985, 8.

8. Playwright Berthold Brecht, for example, when told that Stalin's victims were innocent said, "The more innocent they were, the more they deserved to die." See a review by Herb Grees, *The American Spectator*, May 1986, 46.

9. Howard Snyder, *A Kingdom Manifesto* (Downers Grove, Ill.: InterVarsity Press, 1985), 58.

10. Anthony Campolo, *A Reasonable Faith* (Waco, Tex.: Word Books, 1983) 181.

11. Andrew Kirk, *The Good News of the Kingdom Coming* (Downers Grove, Ill.: InterVarsity Press, 1984), 44. This book was first published in England under the title *A New World Coming*.

12. Sine, *Mustard Seed*, 38.

13. Jim Wallis, "A Painful Alienation," letter to the editor of *Eternity* magazine, March 1985, 68.

14. Ronald J. Sider, interview in *The Wittenburg Door*, October-November 1979, 13.

15. The religious ideologist idealizes Old Testament "structures," which he believes are different, and better, than present democratic, capitalist arrangements. How then can the denunciations of exploitation and oppression in Old Testament prophets such as Amos possibly apply to modern Western democracies? And since oppression and exploitation are "systemic," not individual, why are such prophetic denunciations not considered an indictment of Old Testament "structures" rather than a condemnation of individual actions?

16. Brian Griffiths, *The Creation of Wealth* (Downers Grove, Ill.: InterVarsity Press, 1985), 63. For a full discussion of the Jubilee and Sabbatical Year, see also Ronald Nash, *Social Justice and the Christian Church* (Milford, Mich.: Mott Media, 1983), 77-80.

17. Ronald J. Sider, "Christian Love and Public Policy," *Transformation*, July-September 1985, 14.

18. Ronald J. Sider, *Rich Christians in an Age of Hunger* (Downers Grove, Ill.: InterVarsity Press, 1977), 216.

19. See Thomas Sowell, *Marxism: Philosophy and Economics* (New York: Morrow, 1985), 149. Sowell's book is, among other things, a helpful concordance to the italics-strewn pontifications of Marx.

20. Ronald J. Sider, "An Evangelical Vision for Public Policy," *Transformation*, July-September 1985, 9.
21. Herbert Marcuse is the author of *An Essay On Liberation* (Boston: Beacon Hill Press, 1969), which expounds the idea that all people in advanced Western countries are enslaved by consumerism and that democratic institutions are illusory for this reason. For a helpful discussion of Marcuse's thought see Nash, *Social Justice*, 97-102.
22. Robert Nisbet, *Twilight of Authority* (New York: Oxford University Press, 1975), 249.
23. P. T. Bauer, *Equality, the Third World, and Economic Delusion* (Cambridge: Harvard University Press, 1981), 8.
24. Kenneth Minogue, *Alien Powers: The Pure Theory of Ideology* (New York: St. Martin's, 1985), 194.
25. Carl Sagan might be considered an exception. This writer was happy to hear a man whose proudest possession was a personal letter from Sagan admit that the astronomer was, "the Barry Manilow of Science."
26. Mario Vargas Llosa *The War of the End of the World* (New York: Avon Books, 1984), 310.

CHAPTER 4
THE IDEOLOGICAL MINDSET

THE IDEOLOGICAL SELF-IMAGE

He who has great ideas about running the world should begin
with a small vegetable garden.

(German proverb)

I speak here not of a self-image in the psychological
sense but rather in the moral. But to lapse briefly into psychological language, the self-image in question is healthy indeed. The ideologist "feels good about himself." And he has
solid grounds for feeling this way.

For one thing, he has miraculously escaped all the social conditioning, alienation, and conspiratorial manipulation he sees on every hand: racists, sexists, speciesists,
chauvinists, advertisers, entrepreneurs, the family, servile
academics, and on and on. These have smothered everyone
else in false consciousness (which must be raised); everyone
else lacks true freedom. Since the social theory of the
ideologist portrays society as an oppressive closed system, the
mechanism for the enlightenment of the ideologist must be
some kind of revelation from outside.

For example, Herbert Marcuse thought consumer society enslaved, conditioned, and brainwashed the populace to

such a degree that it would be impossible for people to discover their plight. How, given this total repression, did Marcuse arrive at this theory? He is either a very special person or has received a revelation. Suppose everyone in a society were blind. The critic who said the colors on buildings were garish and should be changed would either have to possess vision or have it revealed to him by an outsider that the color scheme was faulty.

Hence, the ideologist is an oracle, but also a visionary. Here is where ideology takes on remarkable scope and grandeur.

From his perch far above the crass, redneck, manipulated, brainwashed, conservative-voting, free-trading masses, the ideologist reshapes the world with pen and mouth. He deals out restructuring schemes like a croupier does cards. He barks encoded assignments with the confident authority of a quarterback calling an audible at the line of scrimmage, and with the same expectation that there will be no backtalk, just execution.

It all reminds one of a skit performed by Monty Python's Flying Circus, a British satirical troupe often stupid and sophomoric, but on occasion quite incisive. The skit in question was called "How To Do It," a spoof of daytime "educational" talk shows. "Tune in tomorrow," host John Cleese says, "and Jackie will show you how to make black people and white people live together peacefully. Won't that be grand? And then Jackie will show you how to cure all the diseases in the world, and how to play the clarinet. (Jackie: "You just blow through it and wiggle your fingers.") You won't want to miss that." And so on. This is the ideological mode. Everything is possible; it is just a question of getting it done by listening to the right people.

But these metaphors, though helpful, all fall short; the ideological self-image is as close to godlike as anything one can find. It is truly something to behold.

"Let there be Peace," the ideologist says, with a warm glow inside for having so pronounced. "Let there be an end to hunger," too. Now who could argue with that? But in order to accomplish this, another edict must first go out: "To accomplish the Important Things, let there be *massive, global, structural change.*" Yes, this, above all else, as soon as possible. "Let there be an end to selfish nations and nationalism. Let there be global redistribution of wealth." These are sweeping enough, but there is more.

The ideologist invokes not only creatorial prerogatives, but those of punitive justice as well. "You people in those Third World countries—you hurry up with this structural change! Limit those populations, centralize your agriculture! And get rid of your primitive superstitions while you're at it. Do not postpone these measures or we will not give you any food. We mean business here!" This kind of grand strategy, coupled with threats, is the best clue to the ideologist's sense of his own importance and worth.

Needless to say, those who inhabit these lofty regions do not take criticism well. One does not criticize an oracle or god; rather, one learns, obeys, and flatters. The relationship is entirely tutorial. The ideologist is not arguing; he is correcting falsehood with truth. But no fallible human being can be exempt from criticism, especially when advocating utopian measures directly at odds with a free society, and especially when these very measures (such as collectivization of agriculture) have wreaked havoc and death in the past. However, the ideologist counters with a ready explanation—such things are explained as the work of "extremists" and not to be blamed on the new coercive structures themselves.

The ideologist, with support from wherever he can get it, including the Bible, has convinced himself that he is doing The Most Important Thing There Is—that is, Restructuring the World. Without this Restructuring, we will all perish. Whatever his concept of God, the deity is very much dependent on structural, political solutions. The religious ideologist may call these "biblical norms."

Since the ideologist cares so much about Humanity (which is not the same as caring for your neighbor), why then should people disagree with him? "Why are they against me?" he asks. "Don't they know I am right?" Those who question the ideological magisterium can expect to be called names: the wealthy and powerful, court prophets, paid intellectual assassins, reactionaries, bourgeois, fascists,[1] right-wingers, and others.

But there are questions even the ideologist at his loftiest cannot solve. Some sense of mystery remains, but the mystery brings with it a sense of anger. It goes like this: "Since I am sincere and right, why are other people running the world?" In societies that vote in overwhelming numbers for free-market conservatives such as Margaret Thatcher and Ronald Reagan, the ideologist will experience constant frustration. To him it is more evidence that democracy is not working. "Why, just look at how those stupid people vote!" he says to himself. When he sees people eating foods that are not good for them but realizes he is powerless to dictate their diet, this too brings frustration, as does the preference of the masses for football, hockey, and the Indy 500 over a Peace March in protest of nuclear weapons. This frustration may push him into the militant, fundamentalist branch of his *Weltanschauung*—fanaticism.

And what of those other people? What of those uninterested in restructuring their societies and the world? What of the apolitical who perversely pursue careers, develop hobbies, and generally go their own way? What of those Candides and Dr. Panglosses who believe they live in the best of all possible worlds, and even enjoy and celebrate it?

The ideologist must consider such ones apathetic, dupes, sellouts, sham Christians, or persons of moral deficiency. When ideologists gather, Everyman is the butt of many jokes. This too makes the ideologist feel good about himself. In rare cases those who do not fit the ideological profile are considered diseased.[2] Whatever the ideologist thinks of them, they are made to feel miserable at every available opportunity. If the ideologist is a pacifist, as is sometimes the case, it seems as if he, disavowing violence, sets out to nag everyone to death.

Suffice it to say that the self-image of the ideologist is one of moral superiority. This is what he brings to argument, as well as his preformed conclusions. Furthermore, since his ideology places him outside (above) society, he considers it proof of his moral superiority. It is a marvelous circle of reasoning.

THE IDEOLOGICAL TEMPERAMENT

Some years ago, R.C. Sproul wrote a book called *The Psychology of Atheism* (since rereleased under the title, *If There Is a God, Why Are There Atheists?*). Sproul observed that secularism, of which atheism is simply one of the fundamentalist denominations, was forever coming up with various psychologies for religious people. They were "authoritarian" or "rigidly traditional," "dogmatic," or "neurotic" personalities who were simply projecting needs and traits of their own onto something called God, that great Authority Figure in the Sky.

The atheist's question is this: Since there is no God, why are there religious people? One wonders why this question should be of interest; after all, the atheist has no explanation for the entire physical universe. Why should something relatively small like religion be so troubling? But it is, and the question must bother the faithful atheist for a lifetime and, in a sense, lock him into a position of intolerance. As Mort Sahl puts it, the trouble with being an atheist is that you don't get any days off. The atheist must hold that the vast majority of people throughout history have been wrong in their most basic belief in some sort of God. The religionist, on the other hand, may disagree with details of theology or liturgy, but has no basic quarrel with theists of any kind.

Why is there religion? The atheist's answer is that religious believers suffer from some kind of mental illness. They are defective types who need a God to lean on. Given this analysis, it should come as no surprise that, in countries whose creed is atheism, religious believers are tossed into mental institutions to "cure" them.

Sproul simply stood this inquiry on its head: Since there is a God, he asked, why are there atheists? How do we explain them? It is a much more sensible question, since atheists have been a distinct minority throughout history. He then proceeded to analyze the psychology of atheism in terms of trauma, suppression, and substitution. It is a fascinating and audacious study that refuses to accept that any group of people can occupy some remote intellectual precinct where their views are not subjected to the same kind and level of scrutiny they dish out with great vigor.

A full-length professional study is also due for the ideologist. The ideologist explains away promoters of freedom in the same manner that the atheist does the religious believer. Conservative social, political, and economic views are attributed to some personality defect. Some of the labels are the same; the one who talks of freedom in the traditional sense is "reactionary," "insecure," or "authoritarian" ("has a need for law and order and authority figures"). Sometimes he is described as "childish" and "shallow" or, lapsing into moral-theological language, as "materialistic," "greedy," "exploitive," or "vengeful." One also comes across creative designations such as the "marketing mentality" and so on, which are held up as distillations of the most objective and empirical science. It remains for a specialist to work all this out, but a few observations on the ideological temperament are in order.

It is helpful to designate a conservative as someone who has a basic affection and appreciation for his world, that is, his civilization, nation, culture, language, history, tradition, religion, and family. The ideologist, on the other hand, is cut off from the past, which he views as simply a chronicle of oppression continuing into the present, the difference being that now the oppression is hidden behind a facade of freedom. The ideologist considers the things the conservative values as barriers to some Great Unanimity to come. Hence the ideologist must be in some very real sense rootless. The designations of "nativist" for the conservative and "alienist" for the ideologist as developed by Catholic writer Joseph Sobran are helpful.

For all its talk of the free personality, the ideological temperament is actually quite militant and even openly intolerant.[3] Nearly everything he sees—cosmetics, advertisements, fried chicken franchises—is part of the conspiracy of repressive tolerance. One eats a hamburger and is told that this is "bad for you," or that the very act of buying it will cause the death of peasants in the Dominican Republic. One who wants a cup of hot chocolate may be warned that the beverage will only reinforce some rapacious Swiss multinational company that is allegedly practicing genocide in the Third World.

An interesting sidebar to this sort of censoriousness is the Lada automobile, built in the USSR by nonunion labor and sold in Canada and, I am told, soon in the U.S. as well. I have never heard it argued that the purchase of a Lada will only bolster an unjust, rapacious multinational company. This is how former Soviet apologists like Louis Fischer and André Gide describe the USSR—one huge company from which there is no escape and against which there is no right to strike, however poor the wages and conditions. Management sets all wages and always knows best. But of course this company has borders, a flag, a seat at the U.N., and speaks the language of the ideologist. And so, far from being hindered from buying a Lada the way we are Nestle's chocolate or various brands of potato chips, we are positively encouraged to do so, to the point that some ideologists have described the car as being of good quality, which it most emphatically is not. One impartial auto reviewer described it as "a plagiarized Fiat assembled at night." Efficiency and quality—in short, results—matter little to the ideologist. Dogma is paramount: a government, not a private company, makes and profits from the cars, therefore they are good.

The ideologist styles himself as "nonjudgmental," which means in practice that he disbelieves in personal responsibility and blames society as a whole. He talks contantly of "eliminating" and "waging war" on structures he views as harmful. Thus placed, the ideologist is in conflict with just about everything. Mr. Sobran is accurate in describing such ones as "malcontents," because that is what they are. They are the ones who are alienated. What conditions would satisfy them? Or as Sobran also puts it, in what sort of society would *they* be conservatives? That is the enduring question. Although the ideologist wants to "build a new society," he bypasses the stockpile of existing materials. Hence, the dream and the illusion remain supreme.

Isolated, militant, alienated, unable to recognize failure and accept responsibility, constantly blaming and rebuking, forever dreaming; it remains for all this, and more, to be worked out by specialists and published. But we can safely say this much: the ideologist is seldom a pleasant person to be around. In his company, one can fully understand the animus of Frédéric Bastiat, who lived when ideology had just been plucked from reedy minds by political pharaohs and was being groomed to rule, like Moses.

"You who wish to reform everything!" Bastiat said, "Why don't you reform yourselves? That task would be sufficient enough."[4]

THE IDEOLOGIST AND THE OPPRESSED

Though the ideologist considers himself above the masses and is seldom, if ever, a truly poor person, he has needs like anyone else. And in his case these needs are very special and deep. He may consider that the oppressed need him, but the truth is he needs them if his life is to have any meaning at all.

Early in the history of ideology, the oppressed were described as the proletariat, the workers. Cro-Magnon ideologists like Karl Marx claimed special knowledge of the destiny and historical agency of this proletariat. Marxist theory cast the proletariat in the role of the revolutionary instrument. In truth, the vanguard of the revolutions in Europe was composed of intellectuals and renegade bourgeois—even aristocrats—not poor workers. But the ideologist claims to *represent* the workers, and this gives him control over their political meaning. As Muggeridge noted, "A worker is someone for whom everything is done as long as he keeps off stage."[5]

In the West, especially in recent times, Marxist theory is not popular and some have argued that it is a spent force. Others, such as Michael Novak, contend that socialism is dead. Tom Wolfe, examining the leftist (by definition ideological) antibusiness, antiscience, antinuclear banner says, "Socialism remains the goal, of course, but this is not a time in which anyone can present a socialist program by that name."[6] Hence we hear terms such as "industrial policy," and "new world economic order."

But whether this is true or not, current ideologists are most adept at discovering new oppressions and oppressed people, for whom they claim to speak and on whose behalf they act.

Ideologists are seldom elected to anything and rarely participate in elections. Why bother, when the masses are conditioned and manipulated? Ideological representation is really a do-it-yourself process. One simply claims to be a champion of the poor, the hungry, women, homosexuals, and many other miscellaneous minorities, even animals. The minority represented may even be a majority, as in the case of women. However, in the ideological lexicon, "women" generally means, "militant feminists." The ideological system of representation is interesting for several reasons.

In ideological theory, the oppressed owe their awful condition to the determinism of the oppressive structure. They are manipulated, alienated, and imprisoned in traditions and in their own unconscious thoughts. They are slaves of Big Money and evidence that "society is not free." And yet the "oppressors," the "rich and powerful," are outside of these same forces of determinism. They have freedom and power to do and become what they want, but the poor and oppressed do not. Some people are free moral, social, and economic agents; others are not.

By this standard, a middle class person—say, a framing contractor—might owe his condition to hard work, thrift, and a stable family life, coupled with the opportunities afforded by a free market. But a poor person cannot become poor or destitute by anything he does. The middle class person is responsible for his own condition; the poor and oppressed person is not, since it is the oppressive society that makes him that way.

To sum up, the poor are helpless, with no will of their own, without responsibility, and inherently virtuous. The "rich," on the other hand, are willful, active, and inherently villainous.

If the theory was consistent on this point it would have to annul the freedom of the manipulator just as it does that of the manipulated. We would then all be imprisoned in this closed, oppressive system. None of us would ever be able to even diagnose the problem, any more than a deaf society would be able to tell that Julian Lennon and Barry Manilow are singularly untalented musicians. But if we are all free and responsible agents, that shoots down ideological theory; if we are all socially determined, that precludes the possibility of ideologists. Society would be nothing more than a perpetual oppression machine. There is no way around this; one cannot have it both ways.

But this dichotomy, if it can be hidden, offers other advantages. Since the oppressed are victims of forces outside of themselves, they cannot be expected to understand their plight. Someone must do this for them—enter the ideologist.

And since it is contended that our oppressive society gags and censors the ideas of the poor, the oppressed must have someone to both supply them with opinions and agendas, and articulate them in the public forum. The ideologist says, "Here I am, send me," even though he may preceed this with, "Why me, Lord?" He likes to proclaim himself a reluctant champion, drafted by the Downtrodden Masses, who without him would be lost. It is for them, the legend goes, that he strives, and he does not hesitate to let the world know this.

Thus, the ideologist has a vested interest in the inertia and inarticulateness, and even in the continued squalor, of the groups he claims to represent. If they understood their plight and expressed it, the ideologist would be unnecessary. But a member of the allegedly oppressed classes, however poor, who undertakes legitimate political activity and holds opinions contrary to those of the ideologist, disqualifies himself as a constituent. He has failed the consciousness test. It is not enough that he simply be black, Hispanic, a woman, and so on.

For example, suppose a local government wants to attract new industry and offers favorable tax arrangements and other incentives. If a poor Hispanic woman hoping to get a job at one of these new industries were to support the plan, it is doubtful if she would gain much favor with the ideologist who would likely be talking about pollution, the rape of the landscape, and the company's record of military contracts. A black businessman in favor of a new nuclear power plant would quickly lose his status as an ideological constituent, and might even be tagged a "Tom."

A member of a highly visible minority who holds conservative views is to be avoided at all costs, since he is not easily stuffed into the neat category of "blacks." Thomas Sowell, Walter Williams, and Clarence Pendleton are three examples. They are black, highly educated, and articulate . . . gifted at the witty repartee which is the staple of television talk shows, yet one seldom finds them there. They are conservatives; they lack the requisite consciousness. They, and people like them, can speak for themselves, and hence are useless to the ideologist.

For reasons like this, the ideologist describes his constituency in the vaguest possible terms: Third World, Two-Thirds World, Minorities, The Poor, Humanity, Mankind, and so on. The more vague, the more remote and unknown, the more they keep their mouths shut, and as Muggeridge wrote, "stay off stage," the better. The animal-rights crusaders have the ideal situation. Their constituents cannot talk and do not even have to be consulted. It is on their behalf that our awful, meat-eating, "speciesist" society, as animalists have it, is to be restructured into a compulsory vegetarian arrangement.

The ideologist needs the oppressed, not the other way around. The refugee or job-seeker from abroad does not need the Sanctuary worker to enter the United States. Practically anyone who can walk can do this. Rather, the Sanctuary worker needs the illegal alien, through whose plight he can attract media attention and denounce American policy. It is a clear case of exploitation of the poor for political purposes.

An examination of the ideologist's relationship with his constituency shows him to be a freelance ventriloquist constantly auditioning dummy categories, both human and animal, and speaking through whatever he can get. With two of the latest causes being varied forms of sexual deviation and the rights of mice and dogs, the pickings are a bit slim. Perhaps it will soon be claimed that necrophilia is congenital, that necrophiliacs are an oppressed minority, and society must be restructured to make up for past injustices to them. It would not surprise me.

But the Grand March goes on in any case. It remains true that an ideologist without an inert and inarticulate constituency to champion is like a ventriloquist without a dummy.

IDEOLOGICAL LANGUAGE

The ardent effort to discover oppression everywhere involves certain problems of language. Tom Wolfe has described the technique as the "adjective gap" or "adjectival catch-up." Most of the following examples are further explained in his *Intelligent Coed's Guide to America* and *Radical Chic*, highly recommended for everyone whether or not they are radical, chic, intelligent, a coed, or live in America.

Was there real fascism in Europe, with society collectivized around the Great Leader and paunchy brownshirts
terrorizing Jewish shop owners? That may be so, but here
things are just as bad because we allegedly have "social fascism" or "liberal fascism" or "friendly fascism," which turns
out to be an ideological description of a free political system.
This is some *Kristallnacht*.

Is there genuine repression in many parts of the world
in which political activity is forbidden and dissidents jailed
and tortured? Marcuse will tell us that here we have "repressive tolerance," (or as Andrew Kirk has it, "apparent tolerance"). This "repressive tolerance" means the granting of
personal liberty on a massive scale as a clever ruse to disguise
the class struggle, which only socialism *qua* Marcuse can
cure. As everyone knows, making people free and prosperous
is only another example of oppression, and a cruel one at
that. Perhaps General Jaruzelski or Mikhail Gorbachev
could be persuaded to try it instead of telling his comrades to
work harder? If a staunch disciple of Marcuse could convince
either that the granting of personal liberty would only inten-
sify his iron grip of control, who knows? They just might go
for it.

Have there been cases of genocide against Ukranians,
Armenians, Chinese, Jews, and Cambodians in which millions of men, women, and children were murdered for purely
polit ical reasons, often in the name of "building a new society"? Certainly. But as bad as that may be, we in the West
have no right to speak out because here we practice "cultural
genocide." By this is meant, as Wolfe points out, the sort of
thing universities were doing in the sixties. The kids wanted
Meaningful Courses, whereas the universities provided only
learning and preparation for careers, which was Boring. This
is what "cultural genocide" means. That, and allowing huge
revolving red and white chicken buckets to be displayed in
public, which everyone knows is the best way to destroy culture.

Do Marxist governments restrict what may be published by censoring everything that does not coincide with

party dogma and socialist realism? Do they ban a lot of books? Maybe, but here in the repressive West, with its stifling free market approach to publishing, we find "self-censorship." That is, writers—perverse, greedy beings that they are—sometimes produce what is commercially desirable. The American Writers Congress held a conference in 1981 on self-censorship, but it was a nonevent over a noncause. Media attention was then focused on Poland, where real censorship exists.[7]

Is there poverty in much of the globe? Michael Harrington, America's socialist pope, will ignore this and concentrate on "relative poverty" in the United States, where the Health and Human Services budget is bigger than nearly all budgets in the world. The poverty level in the USA is far above the *median income* in many countries, including the USSR. This is "relative poverty."

Was there colonialism, in which European and Asian powers took over vast areas of the world and made them an actual part of the Motherland and Empire? Yes, but today we have "neocolonialism" and "neoimperialism," the great difference being that the new empire, as one writer has it, is "invisible."[8] This would have surprised Lord Kitchener, Cecil Rhodes, and probably Kipling. The idea of an "invisible hand"[9] guiding the free economy troubles the ideologist, but an invisible international empire is acceptable.

Neocolonialism means the condition that exists when any nation sells its goods abroad. This is held to prove that "it needs markets to survive." By this standard, Guatemala is co lonialist because it cannot consume all the bananas it grows and depends on foreign markets; similarly Colombia with its coffee. Tiny Hong Kong, by neocolonial standards, is the most rapacious imperialist power in history.

The irony of this is that the only extant world empire, that of the Soviet Union, is never designated "neocolonial," which is partly accurate because it is simply "colonial." It is the only imperialist power on the scene today. Forget socialism; what they have, they hold.

On the subject of adjectives, the alert reader will be able to find many examples of hagiography. The ideologist bolsters his case by describing books with which he agrees as "brilliant" and people with whom he agrees as "deeply concerned with social justice." In fact, a common form of ideological rhetoric is autohagiography. A writer will describe himself as "deep" and his own books as "brave," which amounts to a glowing review of his own material. Or he may write a highly laudatory autobiography. The hagiography, in all its forms, is the grammatical residue of his high self-image.

Moving on to verbs, the mood is what Minogue calls the "continuous predictive," that dreary prophetic chronicle of gloom, war, and misery that will be our lot if we ignore Structural Change and don't implement world federalism by next Thursday.

Compare this continuous predictive with the subjunctive mood of ideological reverie about the terminus of its activism. The ideologist dreams and says "if only . . ." The word "if" demands the subjunctive, the tense of the *unreal*. Its opposite number is the indicative, which pertains to what *exists*. When explaining about the New Society, of which we are told there are no extant examples, the ideologist sticks with the subjunctive. He may lapse into hyperbole here.

But it is not all rhapsody. There is room too for the imperative. The ideologist gives words such as "should" and "ought" and "must" a vigorous workout. He may not name names, but he points fingers. Here he betrays his self-image.

When addressing the masses the approach is different. In this case things are kept general, full of abstracts such as the poor, the powers, the Third World, North and South (from the "North/South Economic Dialogue"), women, social justice, and other bloodless universalities, as Shiva Naipaul called them. There are no names, no people, and seldom even individual nations, just huge, sweeping categories. These terms are like boxes with false bottoms. You put in what you want, then take it out without being observed.

When talking about society, the ideologist—especially the academic—uses the passive voice whenever possible. Children are taught, decisions are reached, changes are made, viable alternatives are offered, ominous prospects are considered. This use of the passive voice is in direct keeping with ideo logical social theory that depends on structures, not individuals. No one does anything; no one is responsible. Strange, invisible forces must be at work. It is the total society that is oppressive, but no one does anything wrong.

Whenever two or three ideologists are gathered together in the name of Structural Change, and no members of the Oppressor Class or their minions are present, jargon predominates. There are a lot of cliche denigrations: "fascist" is a favorite; "sickies" is another and is used of those awful people who hunt animals (but not for muggers or rapists). "Impact," used as a verb, may also be heard, along with abominations such as "networking."[10]

Ideology is itself an idiom and as Minogue points out it is more difficult to translate into it than out. It is part Newspeak to be sure, but borrows some of the shabbier features of Academic-speak (for example, the excessive use of the passive voice and abstract terms), and Marx-babble. At the same time, it shows a fondness for the subjunctive coupled with strong use of the imperative when any of its spokespersons hold forth from the many bully-pulpits freely available to them today. A hymnwriter once penned, "O For a Thousand Tongues." The ideologist has them and uses them all.

Generally speaking, ideological discourse is too abstract to be compelling. When its rhetoricians do drop the passive, they are too busy telling everyone they are part of the problem and guilty for causing Third World poverty to have much appeal. In fact, ideologists will sometimes preface a speech with: "You are not going to like what I am going to tell you." But given all this, the ideologist has found malleable audiences everywhere. He has learned to handle success.

IDEOLOGICAL ACTIVISM

We have mentioned that the ideologist generally shuns the present political process for various reasons. The religious ideologist considers governments to be part of "the powers" referred to in Ephesians 6:12. It makes no difference whether the government protects freedom or restricts it; if faithful to his dogma he must "oppose the powers" in every case, but does not.

One notes that religious ideologists generally find a candidate to support in American elections. Their enemy is always the conservative—Ronald Reagan for example. I have never heard the Cuban or Nicaraguan governments described as "the powers" and the Christians in those places exhorted to resist them. Practically, "the powers" means Western governments, and being "prophetic" means anti-government action in free states.

But aloofness from electoral politics does not mean that the ideologist is inactive, far from it. He is fond of melodrama and likes to cast himself as a victim. He also enjoys demonstrations, rallies, marches, agitation, consciousness-raising and so on. These have an obvious propaganda purpose but are more important to the ideologist herself than to the spectator. Ideological activism is designed to *make* true what has already been declared to *be* true.

For example, in the sixties, protesters declared that the police were brutal, which they proceeded to prove by baiting them into action, usually by pelting the cops with obscenities and rocks.

Social activist Mitch Snyder declares that the American government allows people to go hungry; then he attempts to starve himself to death to prove it as well as to extort public money for his projects.

Media, especially television news, is quick to pick up on ideological activism. Shouting protesters and clashes with police make an exciting broadcast and good ratings. Joint production of ideological activism is today a growth industry.

CHAPTER 4, NOTES

1. Religious writer Eric Jorstad calls those who oppose the Sanctuary movement, "Christian fascists." See Daniel Ritchie, "Sanctuary," *Eternity*, June 1985, 33.

2. "How many of them [those not in the peace movement] are so afflicted with the *wasting disease of normalcy* that, even as they declare for peace, their hands reach out with an instinctive spasm in the direction of their loved one, in the direction of their comforts, their home, their security, their income, their future, their plans" (italics added). Daniel Berrigan, *No Bars to Manhood* (Garden City, N.Y.: Doubleday, 1970), 57-58; quoted by Ronald J. Sider in *Nuclear Holocaust and Christian Hope* (Downers Grove, Ill.: InterVarsity Press, 1983), 291.

3. "The people who are concerned with social justice can't let people who are not off the hook. Tolerance just won't do." An interview with Ronald J. Sider, *The Wittenburg Door*, October-November 1979, 15.

4. Frederic Bastiat, *The Law* (Irvington-on-Hudson: The Foundation for Economic Education, 1979), 55.

5. Malcolm Muggeridge, *Chronicles of Wasted Time* (New York: Morrow, 1973), 48.

6. Tom Wolfe, "Idea Fashions of the Eighties: After Marx, What?" *Imprimis*, January 1984, 5.

7. Ibid., 4.

8. Jim Wallis, *Agenda for Biblical People* (New York: Harper and Row, 1976), 83.

9. The phrase appears only twice in all of Adam Smith's writings. The context, in *Wealth of Nations*, is the support of domestic industry over foreign.

10. "Megatrends gives me the answer. Both we and the Soviets have hierarchical systems that are outdated. We have to move into networking." Bishop Maurice Dingman in an interview with Dinesh D'Souza, quoted by Michael Scully in "Autumn Scandals," *National Review*, 13 December 1985, 41. Notice the moral symmetry between the USA and USSR and the order in which they are mentioned. Both "systems" are "outdated." "Networking" is simply a buzzword euphemism for a new international "structural" system.

CHAPTER 5
IDEOLOGICAL ARGUMENT

Given the ideologist's unscientific disregard of evidence and his attitude of moral superiority, his arguments will generally take the character of an advancement of dogma through bullying tactics and/or guilt manipulation. In some cases the ideologist simply stands apart from the crowd, turns up the amplifier, and blasts away with volleys of obloquy and agendas of change. But more often he effectively disguises his coercive social evangel as legitimate argument, or resorts to other strategies, often with great success. If these are to be countered, they must be both analysed and recognized.

AD HOMINEM, PETITIO PRINCIPII, AND BEYOND

For example, in keeping with his proclamation of superior moral depth, the ideologist contends that if those on the other side of the argument were as committed and faithful as he, they would of course be following his line of thought and action. This is a modified form of *ad hominem* reasoning; that is, attacking the person one is arguing with rather than his argument. In this case, the opponent lacks certain qualities. "I am deeply committed to economic justice," the ideologist says. "If everyone were as committed

and faithful to economic justice as I, there would be no disagreement. As it is you can't see my point because you are
not as committed as I am. You lack depth." Sometimes it is
put just about that candidly:

> If we were all willing to try as faithfully as we could to be
> shaped by biblical norms about justice and God's concern for
> the poor, then we would be pointed in one direction rather
> than the other.[1]

A variation on this is sometimes encountered in de-
bates about warfare and deterrence. The ideologist is quick
to say that he believes what he does (pacifism or appeasement) because he "cares about humanity," implying that the
other side does not. In fact, it is often baldly stated that the
opponent "lacks compassion." Furthermore, the ideologist
may reinforce this by contending that he cares deeply about
his opponent in the debate. This makes him a kind of
evangelist out to save his opponents from their own views,
which are bad for them and everyone else. It is held out that
if one adopts the views of the speaker, one will thereby not
only be converted to the truth but become in the process a
"caring person." In the case of the religious ideologists the
opponent is given to understand that yielding the argument
will be a way of attaining faithfulness and commitment. The
pitch resembles television commercials for the Marine Corps
in which the prospective recruit is told, "Maybe you can become one of us."

This is an audacious and successful approach, but it is
not argument. It goes beyond *petitio principii*—that is, beg-
ging the question—a strategy in which the conclusion of the
argument is taken for granted in the premises. Rather, it proceeds from the assumption that the opponent is not only
wrong from the outset, but is also a moral and, most likely,
intellectual inferior. The correctness of the conclusion is
taken for granted not only in the premises but because of the
alleged superior character of the ideologist, who believes he
is more deeply committed. Like the pretension to prophet-
hood this conceit—for that is what it is—must be placed in

blind trust before any meaningful debate can take place. But it may be questioned whether meaningful debate is what the ideologist wants.

The pretension to moral superiority, and argument from it, obscures the real point of the debate. To use the example of economic justice once again, the issue may be stated like this: What political and economic arrangements best provide for justice and abundance? The second question dealing with international relations may be phrased: What strategy will maintain international peace? An enormous amount of historical evidence exists on these questions; from study of this evidence we may come to certain conclusions. Nothing is gained by shifting from the validity of the arguments to the character, or lack of it, of the arguers themselves.

What is truly astounding is that this argument from moral superiority has been accepted with the credulity and servility that it has. This widespread tendency to supinely accept moral bullying and *ad hominem* diversions as argument is, in my opinion, one of the main reasons that ideology has gained by leaps and bounds in this century.

The ideologist surveys the pliable and squeamish masses (especially within the church) like French explorer La Vérendrye did the Canadian wilderness. It is likewise virgin territory, populated by cowering natives gone soft as guacamole from easy living, who are often victims of the brain reduction surgery that is the specialty of modern education. Little wonder that the ideologist has been able to plant his flag pretty much wherever he pleases. But the era of exploration and conquest is largely over; we currently live in the heyday of ideological imperialism.

OFFENSE AS DEFENSE

Thus far, the ad hominem nature of ideological argument may be seen in its pretensions of moral superiority. From this superiority it is inferred that the opponent is both wrong and morally inferior. But the opposition—all nonideologists—takes some direct shots as well.

Ideology is a theory of classes and structures which readily assigns all people to one side or the other. One is either part of the problem or part of the solution. Since the ideologist is in favor of structural change, he is likely to add weight to his argument by stating that his opponent is merely an apologist of an oppressive structure, the status quo. This effectively makes the one who disagrees a reactionary, or at least an obstructionist whose purpose must be to protect his own power, wealth, or both, even if he has neither.

Beyond this, the ideologist imputes all kinds of sinister designs to his opponent. Someone makes a proposal for a space-based defense, for example, and it is quickly claimed that he is merely trying to enrich himself and a certain company, or start a war. A politician of conservative inclinations offers a policy to curb violent crime, and we are told that his real intention is to subvert civil liberties or to "turn back the clock" to the dark ages of the garrote and thumbscrew. Let anyone, including strangely enough, feminists, speak out on pornography and they are accused of "trying to force their beliefs on everyone" and of "advocating censorship." Let anyone state that she is less than worshipful of abortion on demand and she is vilified as a defender of patriarchy who "is trying to keep women down." Let a city councilman propose a plan of urban renewal and he is charged with deliberately trying to "displace the urban poor."[2] Medical researchers trying to find cures for leukemia or AIDS are caricatured as wicked, sadistic profiteers who want nothing more than to carve up animals and protect their unjust "speciesist" society.

In practice this works like possessing an unfalsifiable doctrine, for after the wild charge has been made the opponent is then forced to prove that he is *not* up to devious schemes. Add to this the fact that conspiracies and cover-ups do in fact exist in all societies, plus the fact that many people are suspicious of public officials (especially conservatives), and you have a potent strategy indeed. But it is not true argument among moral equals.

The irony is that it is the ideologist who has the sweeping agenda behind his criticism. He maintains the need for structural change; the conservative believes present institutional arrangements are imperfect (as is everything and everyone in this world) but adequate and acceptable because they outperform others and safeguard human rights. It is the ideologist who may harbor coercive designs—for example, his contention that Western societies censor political ideas such as his own. This too has been popping up in religious writing, and it is worthwhile to spend a few minutes examining it.

> Here an interesting fact confronts us: the apparent tolerance of the opinions of others, visible in some capitalist societies, extends to the area of private morals only. . . . The picture changes dramatically, however, in the area of the ethics of economic policies. . . . The illusion of a tolerant, open society goes to the wind.[3]

The author contends that capitalist societies, which he says are "inherently unfair," do not tolerate those critical of the capitalist system. But this contention is not secretly spray-painted on a wall; it is published in book form without censorship, advertised without opposition, and sold everywhere on the open market without fear of confiscation. Indeed, the rights for this book have been picked up overseas in other capitalist countries where the "illusion" of tolerance exists. This is odd behavior for societies that censor all non-capitalist ideas. The notion is falsified by its very utterance.

In reality, what the author means by intolerance is that people do not *accept* his egalitarian, socialist ideas. It is unlikely they don't understand these ideas; it is probable they do and say so, and thus become "mud-slingers" whose "distortion of the views of those who believe that capitalist societies are inherently unfair knows no bounds."[4] Having one's views attacked—the author himself attacks capitalism constantly throughout his book—is not the same as a society that censors all ideological views. Again, the charge is declared false by its very utterance.

But this false claim of intolerance may very well be an advance justification for true censorship and repression if his own soul mates ever take over. Whether this is so or not (in the above case it surely is not), the ideologist stays on the offensive and keeps the pressure on.

I recall a skit on "Saturday Night Live" in which a character was accused of murder. "How do you know he is a murderer?" it was asked. "Well, you never heard him deny it, did you?" This is the way the ideologist argues. And there are more benefits in this plan.

Ever in search of accredited victims of the oppressive status quo, the ideologist can use this strategy to cast himself in this role. Aside from the question of whether his argument has any validity or not, the very fact that his opponent is part of the present political set-up means that the ideologist is, as he likes to put it, being "attacked by the rich and powerful." To anyone who will listen, the ideologist says: "This is not a question of my beliefs or policies. No, they are attacking *me* because my advocacy of the poor and oppressed threatens their wealth and privilege." For example:

> As I listen to the attempts to justify the wealth of rich Christians, it becomes increasingly clear to me that these upper-middle class critics of Sider have *chosen* to interpret the Scripture in a way that allows them to remain comfortable in their riches. . . . [5] (italics added)

This is a classic statement of ideological class analysis. Or, one may find the all-purpose ghost story of "the rise of religious McCarthyism," whose adherents have "made it their business to drive out of the evangelical ranks anyone who does not adhere to this group's particular positions."[6]

It seems strange, given this charge, that the author is being interviewed by an evangelical magazine. He explains in the same interview[7] that he carries on as before, preaching, teaching, making movies, and publishing books. In any case, there is no evangelical pope who can excommunicate anyone. This charge, though quite common, is likewise falsified by its utterance.

McCarthyism was the tactic of a rather unsavory senator and government committee (which included Bobby Kennedy) that accused liberals in the American government of secretly working for Stalin and being members of the Communist party. An "era" has been named for McCarthy even though while he slandered dozens, Stalin slaughtered millions. McCarthyism was, quite properly, rejected by the courts and discarded. There is no parallel between this and private citizens disagreeing over openly published material. In present conditions, it is McCarthyism to accuse someone of McCarthyism.

But by portraying oneself as a victim, argument is transformed into a David and Goliath story or, as Malcolm Muggeridge puts it, a western[8] with good guys and bad guys. Most people naturally pull for the underdog, the little guy, the one in the white hat. For the ideologist, argument becomes a melodrama in which he is in charge of central casting and the script. Ideological Productions, Inc. brings you the True Prophet of the Oppressed, assailed by the rapacious dragon of the Wealthy and Powerful and his McCarthyite Inquisitors. This show is currently serialized everywhere.

THE USE OF SECRETS

There is a sense, linked to the ideological self-image, in which the inner vanguard of those striving to change the structure of society are guardians of secrets. It is possible that they claim to understand the abstruse mysteries of, say, dialectical materialism much better than the camp followers and hangers-on of the movement. This is the gnostic sense of secrecy.

Another possiblity is tactical: the vanguard is privy to certain plans and stratagems that will take place when the Forces of Reaction, as the drama has it, finally resort to open violence against the repressed masses yearning to be free from consumerism, patriarchy, and a huge welfare budget. This private knowledge may find expression as a kind of prophecy. The ideologist in the vanguard may also know certain names of key actors on both sides, and this gives him special elite status and a kind of power.

However, this type of secret knowledge is limited in appeal and restricted in its ability to change entire social structures—which entails changing at least a few people's minds at some point. There must be publicity. It is better for the ideologist to take a different tack with secrecy.

The ideological dictums about liberal Western societies being factories of oppression are secrets in this sense: those allegedly suffering from the oppressions are told about their condition and then informed that this knowledge is something the ruling powers *do not want them to know*. Nearly all of society and tradition then takes on the coloring of a giant repressive conspiracy to keep the ideologist's potential apprentice from knowing the truth about his oppressed condition and seeking liberation through structural change. Common and simple amusements like films and organized sports can be seen as instruments of obfuscation intentionally designed to keep the oppressed from knowledge of their condition. Even Jacques Ellul does this.

Ellul has written sensible and valuable books such as *Betrayal of the West* and *The New Demons*, along with turgid Luddite tracts such as *The Technological Society*. For him, there is a government plot behind video games:

> By that I mean that this is also *a strategy of the government*; if all the citizens are enjoying themselves playing electronic games, rather than thinking about and discussing political issues, the political leaders are completely free to do as they please.[9] (Italics added)

Thus far, at least, all the citizens of France have not chucked politics for PacMan, and even if they did, it is impossible that this would permit the government to do whatever it pleased. The French government of socialist François Mitterand did attempt to take over Catholic schools and was greeted with protesting demonstrators in the millions. The takeover attempt was dropped. So even if video games were, as Ellul says, a secret strategy of the government (perhaps someone on the extreme Left?) they are not doing the job. But there are other villains about.

Religion, especially in its other-worldly dimension, is the *bête noir* of the ideologist. If people patiently accept present conditions in the hope that a better world awaits them in the beyond, it is unlikely, so the reasoning goes, that they will "work for social change." Other-worldly religion is the video game of the people, as a modern Marx might put it.

It should be mentioned that the charge is untrue. The record shows that the most heavenly minded people have done much earthly good. One thinks of medical missions, disaster relief, outreach to alcoholics and lepers, and so on. Of course more could be done, but compared to the accomplishments of ideologists, the magnitude of philanthropic work done by religious people who believe in an afterlife is staggering. The ideologist handles this by maintaining that it is the present "order" and "structure" that needs to be changed. The religious philanthropist, however effective, can be charged with "rearranging deck chairs on the Titanic," or "putting Band-Aids on cancer."

The religious ideologist makes Christianity primarily concerned with altering social conditions. He not only seldom, if ever, mentions the afterlife, but accuses those who preach about it of subverting the true gospel with a "shallow individualism" and "personal salvation." In fact, the religious ideologist often displays an astonishing ferocity against those who talk about heaven a lot. He may have grown up in a fundamentalist church that emphasized this, but he has grown to the point where he considers the social dimension—"the social gospel" if you will—as paramount. Hence, he associates the proponent of an other-worldly evangel with atavism and immaturity. Such a one is a mere marketer of "eternal fire insurance."

But in both cases, the other-worldly dimension works against a raised social consciousness that would shun individualism and strive to change structures. The social message is presented as something the other-worldly religionist and status quo doesn't want anyone to know. Moreover, the Court Prophets and the intellectual assassins of Wealth and Power, we are told, are "worried" about the "forces of change."[10]

The use of secrecy in this sense can be a powerful proof text for the initiated and apprentice alike. In whatever form they appear, secrets have always had tremendous appeal. In this case, the changer of society considers himself a special person with special knowledge; the objects of his recruitment are led to believe they have inside knowledge of social forces which the powers that be do not want them to have. The plainly observable fact that in Western countries anything may be published and propagated is no obstacle to this kind of "secret." Neither is the evident truth that dissent is not suppressed. Thus the ideologist again gets to have it both ways. He can be public and secret at the same time.

AUTHORITY

Ideologists are often name-droppers and like to play up their academic credentials to lend weight to their arguments. They are used to talking down to people, and they are by no means alone in this respect. But ideologists often play fast and loose with the whole concept of authority. They both deny it and appeal to it when it suits their purposes.

The secular ideologist may contend that "he is on the right side of history," which in this case means the future. The concept bears no resemblance to what history is: that branch of human knowledge dealing with the affairs and events of the past. For the ideologist, history takes on almost personal connotations, an ersatz deity on whose right side one may or may not be. Who says the ideologist is right? History does. History is said to have decreed that the good guys will win, as though it were a matter of record. This is secular eschatology in its most blatant form. What better way to disguise it than to call it History?

The religious ideologist appeals to the Bible to baptize both his diagnosis of structural evil and his remedy of social change. His success with religious audiences, who accept scriptural authority, very much depends on how well he can present his vision as "taught in the Bible."

One easy way to do this is to simply tell the audience that what you are doing is a "biblical study" or that your book falls under the rubric of "practical theology," a claim made for *Rich Christians in an Age of Hunger.*[11] A number of books present an ideological agenda as a version of God's kingdom.[12] This is sometimes enough to get the job done.

But since the societies described in the Bible were ancient and agrarian, it is futile to canvass the Scriptures to find working models for modern nation states. Even Ron Sider says "The Bible does not have an economic blueprint for the modern economy or a political platform for the next presidential candidate."[13] All one can do is try and deduce some general principles from the text and apply them to modern situations. The societal instructions given to Moses and the Israelite kings are no more normative for modern cultures than God's directive to Abram to "get thee hence to a land I will show thee" means that the contemporary reader should sell his house and move to Iraq. He should, though, be living in obedience to God, as Abram did. The Scriptures are interpreted in their historical context then applied to modern situations. Interpretation and application should not be confused, as they often are.

Since even the religious ideologist may agree that we are not to try and restructure, say, Manitoba on the lines of Old Testament Judah, his appeal to the authority of the Bible may take a different form.

For example, in his effort to prove that capitalism, as it exists in the West, is not only bad and exploitive but that God himself hates it, the ideologist mixes his syllogism:

> Major Premise: God hates injustice. Minor Premise: Capitalism is unjust. Conclusion: God hates capitalism.[14]

The major premise is taken from the Bible and is something on which all Christians agree. The minor premise, however, is drawn not from the Bible but from empirical observation and is a conclusion in itself. The truth or falsity of it cannot be established by the major premise, however loudly or often it is repeated. Hence the conclusion—God hates capitalism—doesn't follow and is taken for granted in the premises, a clear case of *petitio principii*. This of course is the very essence of ideology, and the authority of the Bible is easily conscripted.

If the religious ideologist can persuade an audience that his vision and that of the Bible are the same, then the one who has a different vision more in line with the free principles of the status quo may be perceived or labeled as "denying the Bible." The one who does not attempt to prooftext his policies from the Pentateuch may even be decried as a humanist or one whose major influence is not the Bible but the Enlightenment or some political party. The ideologist of course considers himself and his program of change a model of biblical fidelity and does a lot of prooftexting. His books are more likely to have an index of biblical quotations than a standard index, which gives the work the appearance of theology.

With Christian people whose life is built around obedience to the authority of Scripture, this is a most effective approach. Ideologists have been very successful at portraying their agenda as scriptural or what God is doing in the world. It has carried the day for them on many occasions.

The defender of free market capitalism does not try to make this system of political economy the kingdom of God and, in fact, says plainly that it is not.[15] He can point to general principles in the Bible that are part of his system: private ownership of property, the freedom to buy and sell, and so on. He can also point to the record of this system in providing for human need, something acknowledged even by Karl Marx. But when this happens, the ideologist's distaste for evidence becomes apparent by another strange use of authority. Consider this statement for example: "The fact that capitalism is better than all other systems doesn't mean it's the system that Jesus approves of."[16] Divine authority is used to sunder measureable results and performance from divine approval. The ideologist's system thus does not have to work well to be the one "Jesus approves of." Jesus, apparently, doesn't care if it works well or not, an unlikely enough attitude even in his human trade of carpenter. What system does Jesus approve of? None is named. Here the religious ideologist is always vague and often utopian; there are no extant models of his principles. This is a form of gnosticism.

I take another example of ideological ambivalence toward authority from my own experience. One man wrote to me objecting most strongly to my contention in *The Generation That Knew Not Josef* that the Soviet Union is a repressive, expansionist, totalitarian state. After being told up front that I was wrong and that the writer was a scientist who "cared about humanity," and was "concerned" about me (all classic nonarguments), I was informed in no uncertain terms that my argument depended too much on "authority figures." By this he meant people I had cited such as Malcolm Muggeridge, Arthur Koestler, André Gide, and Aleksandr Solzhenitsyn, among other writers and journalists who actually spent time in the USSR and were witnesses to monstrous acts of tyranny, including genocide.

Questions involving life and death are usually decided by the courts. In this forum, eyewitnesses are most important since not everyone can be in the same place at the same time, and for other reasons which will be obvious to almost everyone. If some famous, bestselling author and psychologist were to intervene in the judicial process and proclaim that, in her opinion, the accused was guilty or not guilty, and if the jury and populace accepted this because of the fame and reputation of the psychologist, this might be accurately described as a false verdict based on an authority figure. The only special authority of the eyewitnesses is that they saw the crime. Their testimony is empirical evidence that is accepted by all civilized courts. Hearsay evidence and personal opinion are nowhere accepted by the same.

Having told me that my argument depended on authority figures, the writer then proceeded to inform me, without any embarrassment whatsoever, that the USSR was "more peaceful" than the United States and NATO. How did he know this? *The United Nations said so*, he said, though he cited no specific statement of any UN member or body. It was all truly astonishing. Somehow, the United Nations is not supposed to be construed as an authority figure. This august body has proclaimed that a homeland for Jews constitutes racial discrimination (the infamous resolution "Zionism is a form of racism"). One wonders how the gentleman who wrote me accepts this authoritarian dictum. Is it true because the U.N. said so?

At no point, I should add, was any specific data about the USSR proffered by my critic; no mention of internal passports, atheistic indoctrination, the illegality of all parties except the Communist party, of all philosophies except Marxism-Leninism, of restrictive emigration policies, mass murder, tossing of dissidents into labor camps and insane asylums, and so on. None of this exists in the United States, Canada, or any Western democracy. Raymond Aron, examining the evidence in the fifties, noted that Soviet and American society were the "exact opposite," on virtually every point.[17] I cite this to show how the ideological method of argument obscures the issues. In this case the facts were getting in the way of the ideologist's contention that he is right *a priori* and more humanitarian than his foe.

Furthermore, I was sent a booklet about the nuclear freeze movement written by someone the writer ostensibly held to be an authority on the subject. So the ideologist will cite authorities even as he discounts another argument for being based, as he sees it, on authority figures.

My sin, of course, had been to cite the USSR as repressive. Ideological dogma has it that, far from this being the case, the United States and other Western societies are the real culprits, the truly repressive societies. The ideologist holds to the moral symmetry theory, that there is nothing to choose between the "superpowers." So acute is his ideological retinitus pigmentosa, that he cannot see any difference between countries surrounded by barbed wire and countries full of immigrants.

One writer has found a handy way around this by including the USSR in denunciations of "Western" aggression.[18] This would surprise Mr. Gorbachev, and even violates geography, but then, the Soviets were not included in the North/South Economic Dialogue either. Australia, far to the south, was included, but it had to be classified "North." Things are indeed a mess.

I AM THE PROOF, YOU ARE THE PROOF, WE ARE THE PROOF

The ideologist also uses a strategy of argument similar to one advocated by some American politicians in the early seventies regarding Vietnam: "Let's say we won, then get out." When the ideologist cannot carry the day in reasonable debate, with empirical arguments, or with authority, he turns to the tactic of making himself a proof.

This is not in the sense of moral superiority we discussed earlier. Rather, it is based on the ideologist's tendency to take inevitable imperfection—which is the lot of human life on this earth—as an argument for structural change. He does this even if experience shows that structural change of the type he advocates has made conditions worse, not better, in the past. This does not appear to matter.

In this case, the fact that the ideologist is deeply upset at the condition of things is used in this manner: "I may not be right, but it is significant in itself that I am not satisfied with present arrangements. My very discontent shows there is something wrong with the system." In other words, "You may argue very well, but how do you explain *me*?" The ideologist thus becomes his own symptom and proof text, a most convenient position indeed. There he is; you cannot get rid of him.

A prominent Christian educator uses a similar method to make the case for pacifism. He acknowledges that he is an "ardent idealist" and that his pacifism was "not logically reasoned out. Neither was it biblically based"[19] (two astonishing and fatal admissions). We are left with the fact that he is both a Christian and pacifist and remained so through World War II, as if this in itself not only had great bearing on the whole debate but should be enough to settle the issue. This case, and others like it, show how easily religious people of an ideological bent can substitute personal experience for analysis, evidence, and argument. They want to resolve the question at hand not in a debate but in a testimony meeting. Should a Christian be a pacifist? "Well," says this man, "*I* am." Meeting adjourned.

The confessional can also be pressed into service. A popular writer and lecturer holds up the Bible as the standard of right and wrong, with an important qualification: "However, there are Marxist Christians who quickly point out that my approach is far too simplistic." [20]

The writer uses his confession of being simplistic as a partial endorsement of Marxist class theory. At the end of the paragraph, he says, "Increasingly, I find evidence to support this Marxist claim." This is reasonable, since he has cited himself as part of the evidence. He has proved his contention right by confessing to a lesser wrong. As to the question whether a Christian can or should be Marxist or use Marxist analysis,[21] that appears to be assumed up front. In any case the names of these Marxist Christians are not revealed, so we are unable to pursue the matter on a personal basis.

Moving from Marxism to feminism, consider this:

> Christians should be ardent feminists. There is so much unconscious sexism in my statements that sisters in the Lord are constantly pointing it out to me. It is one more way in which the culture influences us without our even knowing it.[22]

A number of interesting things are happening here. First, the bold imperative in the opening sentence: Christians should not only be feminists, but ardent feminists. Really? Like Betty Friedan or Gloria Steinem? Next, the "unconscious sexism" in the writer himself, which both baptizes the "sexist" analysis and holds the author up as symptom and proof of his own argument. He is making the case for feminism by confessing to sins of sexist language, which are nevertheless not deliberate but unconscious, thus resolving him of responsibility. We are reminded again of the mysterious, manipulative structures of our culture, which the feminists have discovered and which are ultimately responsible for this unconscious sexism. Radical feminists would add that until the whole culture is structurally altered, nothing will change. This is textbook ideological argument and posturing.

To the discontented potential ideologist, the personal proof approach can also be a powerful tactic. A woman preyed upon by feminists may find herself, quite naturally, slipping into "traditional" roles and mannerisms—and even dress—which the ideologist considers to be badges of oppression. This personal backsliding can easily become a proof text for the contention that all of society is intentionally designed to keep women down. Her own behavior becomes evidence that "they must be right."

In similar style, the heavy imposition of guilt so typical of the religious ideologist can be proffered as a proof text. If the message makes people uncomfortable, it is held that this is a great proof of its correctness. After all, it is argued, Jesus never made people comfortable. "Tolerance won't do," says one writer, "the kind of tension [feelings of guilt] is inherent in the message."[23] By implication, then, those not working for structural change are simply preaching what people want to hear and helping "unjust rich folk"[24] justify their wealth and power. The message is an effective way to elicit guilt.

At this point, the question in the listener becomes, "How can I get rid of this guilt?" The ideologist is right there with his agenda of activism. This, he says, will do the trick.

But the religious ideologist may grow uncomfortable with constantly bewailing the state of everything and the malignancy of the Government. He may not like the association that comes from always pointing the finger and "being the heavy,"[25] so he may momentarily abandon his elevated platform and temporarily join the ranks of the guilty. He temporarily becomes part of "the powers" that are normally to be opposed. This posture can take the form of the national repentance spoken of by C.S. Lewis. The ideologist is still on the attack but simply changes the "you" to "we," and, having switched to "we," he may say what he pleases. As Lewis put it:

> By use of a dangerous figure of speech, he calls the Government not "they" but "we." And since, as penitents, we are not encouraged to be charitable to our own sins, nor to give ourselves the benefit of any doubt, a Government which is called "we" is *ipso facto* placed beyond the sphere of charity or even of justice. You can say anything you please about it. You can indulge in the popular vice of detraction without restraint, and yet feel all the time that you are practising contrition.[26]

Thus, by all these devices, the ideologist seeks to put himself in a can't-lose situation. He has often pulled it off. Me, you, we—all of us make his case one way or another. In this sense at least, he believes in people.

THE GRAND MARCH OF PROGRESS

It should be remembered at the outset of this section that the ideologist considers the past nothing more than a chronicle of oppression. Consider the clarity and sweeping dogmatism of this statement by Janet Richards:

> The facts are stark, but beyond any question. All social arrangements, institutions, and customs were designed to ensure that women should be in the power and service of men. This no doubt sounds like pure feminist rant, but it is not.[27]

Just what the theory that *all* social institutions were for the express purpose of oppressing women might be is difficult to say. It is certainly not scholarship, nor history. Pure feminist rant, in fact, probably comes closest.

In pure Marxist rant, all customs and institutions were designed to oppress the workers. All ideologists look backward for barbarism, forward for civilization; backward for oppression, forward for liberation. They are, in a word, progressive.

In the twentieth century, which has such distaste for thought, the simpler an idea the better the possibilities for its adoption. Perhaps the simplest of all ideological arguments is the one from chronology. The correctness of an idea is judged by whether it is progressive or not. As the theory has it, whatever comes later is both better and right. Robert Nisbet comments:

> No dogma or superstition in any religion yet uncovered by anthropologists is more tyrannizing and also more intellectually absurd than that of the historically necessary. But it is this dogma nevertheless that has had the greatest appeal to several generations of intellectuals bereft of religion and driven thereby into the arms of the waiting church of historical necessity.[28]

The ideologist has appropriated the magic word of professional advertisers—*New!* Yet ideological schemes are really not new at all but simply feudalism expressed in Newspeak. (More on this later.) Of course we are also told that the New Society will be not only new but *Improved!* The jury is out on both scores.

By the chronological standard, American teetotalers could have claimed progressive status for Prohibition. It was, in fact, a progressive issue. Those who were against it could have been easily described as anarchical enemies of social health and progress who "wanted to turn back the clock" to the dark days when booze was available on every hand. Doubtless they were often so described.

The great advantage of the progressive view is that one's opponent is then easily considered to be an atavist, a defender of the past. He may also be on the wrong side of history. The progressive on the other hand is for the future, by which he means the sparkling version found in his beatific vision. It is *jamais vu* over *déjà vu*. This is far from merely a secular idea; religious writings have baptized it as well.[29]

The chronological or progressive standard proceeds from a view of history that Czech novelist Milan Kundera calls The Grand March:

> The Grand March is the splendid march on the road to brotherhood, equality, justice, and happiness; it goes on and on obstacles notwithstanding, for obstacles there must be if the march is to be the Grand March.[30]

Kundera describes this Grand March as both a "fantasy" and a "kitsch." The ideologist, religious and secular, may not be at the head of the procession, but either tags or goose-steps along in this parade, depending on his level of raised consciousness. His great genius is to integrate everything—sociology, Christianity, racquetball, hamburgers, video games, anything—into this Grand March. Those not in the procession backslide inexorably into the past, which is where free enterprise democracy is found. They are "out of step with history," or "destined for the dustbin of history."

With the destination of the Grand March so desirable, the obstacles must not be allowed to hinder progress. This is often true even if these obstacles are human beings. Sabina, one of Kundera's characters, has been trampled by the March. Her country has been invaded. What does she think of this?

> She would have liked to tell them that behind Communism, Fascism, behind all occupations and invasions lurks a more basic, pervasive evil and that the image of that evil was a parade of people marching by with raised fists and shouting identical syllables in unison. But she knew she would never be able to make them understand.[31]

One understands just how Sabina felt when one tries to explain to an ideologist why the progressive standard of right and wrong is invalid.

WORDS AND MEANING

When the ideologist—generally by status or trade an intellectual—is faced with an uncomfortable consequence of his plain statements, he resorts to saying that the normal, grammatical sense of his words was not what he meant. He also does this when things do not turn out as planned.

For example, in Leninist theory the state is identified with the bureaucracy and the army, and the whole entity is described as a parasitic monster that "chokes the pores" of society. But as Kenneth Minogue explains:

> Lenin didn't really mean it either, since within months rather than years, he was reconstituting a state apparatus of his own, including bureaucracy, army and secret police, which has presumably been choking a lot of vital pores ever since.[32]

Feminists have invested a lot of emotion and rhetoric in an idea called comparable worth, which contends that free market arrangements are unjust in determining what people are to be paid. This is to be adjudicated another way. But how? There is simply no way, other than the establishment of a huge bureaucracy in charge of determining fair wages, for the idea to be implemented. It would require the destruction of a free market society, something many feminists openly espouse. Militant feminism is the women's auxiliary of socialism.

"But you misunderstand," some feminists tell us. "By comparable worth we don't mean to advocate a huge bureaucracy. That's not what we mean at all." They want their program somehow implemented with no adverse consequences. But telling the world they don't mean this cannot remove the consequences. This is a plea for everyone to judge the program by its good intentions, and this will not do. The ideologist will never judge the conservative on his intentions, but rather assumes they are malign.

Take the endlessly repeated notion that for social justice to be achieved and hunger to be alleviated, wealth must be redistributed on a global scale. On a practical level, massive redistribution of wealth requires central control of economies. It requires coercion. There is no way around this.

For example, suppose a militant redistributionist with good intentions—let us call him the Hunger Czar—were in charge of the American economy and told a farmer to stop growing feed crops for meat production. Aside from the issue of whether he would be right or wrong to do this, what if the farmer refuses to do so? What if he maintains that he will grow only what he wants and sell to whom he wants? What will the Czar do? Will he imprison the farmer and confiscate his land? And what if thousands of farmers take the same stance? The Czar must force them by police power to do what he wants. It will be a messy scene indeed.

In the past, rulers such as Stalin have simply killed independent farmers by the millions. This action was applauded and defended by ideological clergy of the day. But even if such coercion is what the ideologist has in mind, he is quick to point out that it is not what he means. No, he didn't mean that, and in fact he is against coercion and "opposed to socialism." But if he allows free principles to prevail, his redistribution system cannot work and is reduced to rhetoric about what should be done. If he offers voluntary incentives, this can hardly be described as redistribution. Does the ideologist, when he advocates redistribution, mean coercion? He often tells us that he does not. This leaves the observer puzzled to say the least. Probably what the ideologist has in mind is the beatific destination of Kundera's Grand March, but we never know for sure. All that remains absolutely certain is that the ideologist is most upset with the state of things.

The "I didn't mean it" ruse is a form of gnosticism that

throws us back to the ideological claim of moral superiority as proof of the correctness of their argument. Thick books full of plain grammatical statements advocating sweeping social change, economic centralization, and military surrender are apparently unreliable guides. We must look to the ideologist for an *ex cathedra* interpretation, and trust that he means well, which is how many people, unfortunately, evaluate him. The more pressing question is how the sort of policies he advocates have fared in the past. The ideologist judges free societies on their worst cases, not their claims, but he wants to be judged by his rhetoric, not the past performance of the kind of policies he espouses.

Take too the most common justification of the religious ideologist for a coercive economic arrangement: "God is on the side of the poor." Does this mean that God encourages people to *seek* poverty for themselves and their families? This is denied for obvious reasons. Does it mean that to be poor is to be a Christian? Even Ronald J. Sider says no.[33] He is quicker, like others who take this line, to explain what this slogan—for that is what it is—does *not* mean than what it does. Does God care more about the salvation of the poor than the middle class or any other class? No, the Bible says that God is not a respecter of persons. What, then, is the meaning of "God is on the side of the poor?" One suspects it can change at any time.

Turning to literature, one remembers the pigs in George Orwell's *Animal Farm* who were constantly changing the Seven Commandments as it suited them. The liberated animals, especially Boxer the horse, the most sympathetic character in the story, were puzzled to say the least.

Pop culture also provides an illustration of the whole strategy under discussion. Gilda Radner used to play a character called Emily Latella on "Saturday Night Live." Emily was a commentator on the evening news and was always upset about something, the kind of lady who writes angry letters to the editor. She had heard that someone had proposed that Puerto Rico be turned into a "steak," and ranted and

raved about this for five minutes at high levels of righteous
indignation. She was deeply concerned about it—probably
a vegetarian. When informed by a frustrated Jane Curtin
that her whole position was based on a misnomer, that the
resolution had to do with Puerto Rico being turned into a
state not a steak, she turns to the camera, smiles and says,
"Never mind." Momentarily abashed, she was always back
next week for another crusade.

This is how the ideologist argues. When it is shown
that his position is much ado about nothing, or that one of
his major premises is faulty or ill-defined, or that his schemes
would require coercion, he says, "Never mind. I didn't mean
it." But he, like Emily, quickly climbs back onto Rosinante
and joins the vanguard that prowls free societies in search of
the downtrodden and oppressed.

SPECIAL PRIVILEGE

It has been mentioned that the ideologist cannot abide
criticism. The social critic of an ideological cast considers it
an act of outrageous gaucherie for anyone to criticize those
who are already critical. To debunk a debunker is considered
impossible. Those who do this are thought to be self-
interested defenders of the status quo—the rich and powerful
or their toadies—who are pleading on behalf of an oppressive
orthodoxy. The ideologist, accordingly, wants critical immunity, to be above reproach.

And he has, in fact, been accorded sacred cow status.
When has anyone seen a five-part investigative series on the
Green Peace organization or Ralph Nader? How about a PBS
documentary on the politics of the ACLU? Just how is
Mother Jones magazine funded? Can Mike Wallace tell us
that? What about the Institute for Policy Studies? Is it, like
the Brooklyn Bridge, suspended by cables? Or how about a
report on the salaries and charitable donations of Physicians
for Social Responsibility and myriads of other "concerned"
groups? How much of this concern actually trickles down to
the supposed beneficiaries? Far from ever being criticized,
groups such as these are positively venerated by media

people. This is both sad and unjust, but the situation is every bit as bad in the religious community.

England once practiced something called the Benefit of Clergy. Under this arrangement ministers were above prosecution. This caused much mischief, not to mention injustice. Today we have an unwritten version called the Benefit of Prophets. Those who consider themselves, or are considered by others, to be prophets are thought to be beyond criticism. However wild, impractical, or farfetched their statements, we are told they mean well or that "their hearts are in the right place," and we are not to bother them, nor may we criticize their published writings. If anything, we are urged to provide a platform from which they can propagate their ideas.

Sanctuary workers on trial for violating American immigration laws demand special treatment for their allegedly religious motives. The real question is: Was the law broken? Clerical collars and high motives do not place one above the law. Many people are in the business of smuggling aliens. Sun Yung Moon received no special treatment in his tax case, and Sanctuary workers should not either. Theirs is a strange martyrdom; they want to be a victim and let off at the same time.

Should anyone criticize the religious ideologist, he turns to piety for a defense: "Why are you criticizing your brother in Christ?" The one who had been a Court Prophet of the Church of Caesar and a defender of Unjust Wealth is suddenly a brother to be entreated. "Why are you bearing false witness? Don't you know what I really meant?" People who publish and lecture in the public forum and advocate the massive restructuring of free societies cannot, by this feeble device, escape critical evaluation of their ideas. These issues are not questions for a testimony session or a deacon's meeting. It is a poorly disguised plea for special treatment. People who pronounce loudly and dogmatically on global issues and who urge policies that have deprived millions of freedom and have caused massive death and destruction in the past should expect to be severely and regularly criticized.

Now if someone had written that, say, the leaders of Christians for Socialism[34] or a similar group were all wicked or unkind to animals, were transvestites or homosexuals, then the pietistic defense might have some meaning. An apology would be in order. But as a retreat from critical evaluation, it is invalid. Religious ideologists also have other methods.

The religious ideologist is eager to speak at forums whose agenda is set by people like himself, and whose platform and audience jostle with soul mates—kind of a combined studio audience and laugh/applause track. He likes the home-court advantage. These affairs sometimes feature much wrangling about the wording of statements on important subjects like Peace and Poverty. There is much behind-the-scenes debate and rumors as to who will sign what, and so on. But the documents, like grandiose U.N. pronouncements, are generally read by few and heeded by none. The events themselves tend to be more agitprop theatre than anything else. But the ideologist has a fondness for drama reflected in his participation in demonstrations. He often co-produces these affairs, then stars in them. If a book and speaking engagements can come out of it, so much the better.

To me these strategies are all declarations of the bankruptcy of ideological argument, which is not really argument at all but a form of power posturing, bullying, and guilt manipulation coupled with pleas for special treatment that the ideologist is never willing to accord anyone else. There is another tactic that deserves separate mention.

TU QUOQUE

The distinguishing feature of traditional liberalism—what is now called conservatism—is its lack of ideology. That is, it does not call for structural change. It views the institutions of a limited government, democratic polity, cultural pluralism, and free market economy, which were themselves a response to authoritarian government, not as the Kingdom of God but as an arrangement that outperforms all others and maintains freedom. In fact, it is the religious ideologist who claims his ideas are taught in the Bible and equates his vision with the Kingdom of God, as the titles of many books on Christian social policy attest. This is why he is so hard on his religious opponents; they are not just wrong, they must be *heretics*. They are held to be fighting God himself and preaching a false, shallow gospel.

The conservative does not want structural change, particularly rapid change, which he views as always harmful. The phrase "conservative ideology" is an oxymoron. Absence of ideology is what defines conservatism. And yet the ideologist never hesitates to describe the conservative as an ideologist.

> Ideology is an attempt to defend rationally the vested interests of a group who control power in society. It acts like a guard-dog trained to spring at the throat of an intruder.[35]

This description is pure class theory, which is what ideology is. The approach is a *tu quoque*—"you too"—a retort. What better tactic than to entangle the opponent in his own accusation? This is most often employed by children and is the last line of ideological defense.

CHAPTER 5, NOTES
 1. Interview with Ronald J. Sider in *The Wittenburg Door*, October-November 1979, 13.
 2. The same people who now "displace the urban poor" were accused of "white flight" some years ago. To move back to the inner city from the suburbs is called "gentrification."
 3. Andrew Kirk, *The Good News of the Kingdom Coming* (Downers Grove, Ill.: InterVarsity Press, 1984), 77-78.
 4. Ibid., 78.
 5. Anthony Campolo, *A Reasonable Faith* (Waco, Tex.: Word Books, 1983), 144.
 6. Interview with Anthony Campolo in *The Wittenburg Door*, June-July 1985, 15.
 7. Ibid., 31.
 8. See Malcolm Muggeridge, *Chronicles of Wasted Time*, vol. 1 (New York: Morrow, 1973), 160. Muggeridge says anyone can be an instant success as a commentator as long as he portrays political situations as westerns, with good guys versus bad guys.
 9. An interview with Jacques Ellul, *Presbyterian Journal*, 1 January 1986, 7.
10. Jim Wallis, "A Dream," *The Wittenburg Door*, August-September 1982, 27, 28. The phrase, "the government is worried" appears three times.

130 IDEOLOGY: A THREAT TO FREEDOM

11. See the entry for InterVarsity Press in the 1983 *Writers' Market* (Cincinnati: Writer's Digest Books, 1982), 86.
12. Some recent examples: *A Kingdom Manifesto* by Howard Snyder and *The Good News of the Kingdom Coming* by Andrew Kirk. Jim Wallis moved from *Agenda for Biblical People* to *A Call to Conversion*.
13. Sider, *Wittenburg Door*, 15.
14. I owe this formulation to Kenneth Myers.
15. Michael Novak, for example, states that democratic capitalism is "not the Kingdom of God." See Novak's *Spirit of Democratic Capitalism* (New York: Simon and Schuster, 1982), 21.
16. Interview with Anthony Campolo, *Contemporary Christian Magazine*, August 1984, 28.
17. Raymond Aron, *The Century of Total War* (New York: Beacon Press, 1955), 357.
18. Kirk, *Kingdom Coming*, 35.
19. Vernon Grounds, "A Peace Lover's Pilgrimage," *Perspectives on Peacemaking*, John Bernbaum ed. (Ventura, Calif.: Regal Books, 1984), 164.
20. Campolo, *Reasonable Faith*, 142.
21. I have often heard it contended that using Marxist analysis does not make one a Marxist. This raises an important question: Could one have used National Socialist (Nazi) racial analysis and not in some meaningful sense been a Na- tional Socialist? Could there have been a "Nazi-Christian dialogue"?
22. Campolo, *Contemporary Christian*, 28.
23. Sider, *Wittenburg Door*, 15.
24. Ibid.
25. Ideological writers are aware of this problem. I am informed that a writer of baleful tomes about the future is studying the works of Erma Bombeck in order to add a light touch. Any book that results is one I want to see.
26. C.S. Lewis, "The Dangers of National Repentance" in *God in the Dock*, Walter Hooper ed. (Grand Rapids, Mich.: Wm. B. Eerdmans, 1970), 190.
27. Janet Richards, quoted by Michael Levin in *New Perspectives, U.S. Commission on Civil Rights*, Fall 1985, 40.
28. Robert Nisbet, *Twilight of Authority* (New York: Oxford University Press, 1975), 235.
29. For example, in *The Good News of the Kingdom Coming* (originally *A New World Coming*) one comes across chapter titles such as: "Emigration from the Old World" and "The Glories and Follies of a Passing Age." The assumption is that statist principles are inexorably replacing those of the free market.
30. Milan Kundera, *The Unbearable Lightness of Being* (New York: Harper Col- ophon, 1984), 257.
31. Ibid., 100.
32. Kenneth Minogue, *Alien Powers: The Pure Theory of Ideology* (New York: St. Martins, 1985), 202.
33. For a full discussion of "God is on the side of the poor," see Ronald Nash, *Social Justice and the Christian Church* (Milford, Mich.: Mott Media, 1983), 161-68.
34. Christians for Socialism is a Detroit-based group. The June 1982 issue of *The Other Side* magazine describes it as "an independent movement committed to class struggle in support of poor and working people" (p. 21). If all ideological groups would be so candid in their taxonomy, much confusion would be re- lieved.
35. Kirk, *Kingdom Coming*, 61-62.

CHAPTER 6
THE CONSEQUENCES OF IDEOLOGY

Like falling ash from Mount Saint Helens, ideology settles on everything. It blurs, chokes, enrages, and generally makes a mess of things. The trade winds of mass media, the academy, and even at times the arts, spread it everywhere. Its great discovery is that the freest, most prosperous societies in history and the principles on which they are based are just a facade covering a reality of horrible oppression.

In its pure, secular form, ideology is Christianity's greatest competitor since it rejects individual moral agency and responsibility. It ridicules the idea of heaven as a narcotic against change but promises pie on the earth by and by—just around the corner, in fact. In its popular form, which has been picked up wholesale by religious activists, ideology is freedom's greatest competitor. Of that there can be no doubt since it calls "alienation" what most people call "freedom." Most people cherish what the ideologist despises.

Whatever the ideologist denounces, whatever group he champions, whatever social vision he holds out to the masses, he remains consistent in denying that free economic and political arrangements as they presently exist in the West are desirable. Not only so, but they constitute the greatest repression of all time. If the world is to be restructured according to ideological doctrine, free societies would have to go.

The ideologist hates free societies primarily because people in them have no obligation either to listen to or obey him and perversely spend much of their time in activities which the ideologist thinks are not good for them. Usually drawn from the ranks of higher education, the ideologist is used to giving dictation and wishes to extend this function from the classroom and laboratory to society and the world. It is the power to design and restructure he is after, and freedom in its traditional sense can only be an obstacle. Ideology is at bottom a power theory.

For this reason one can never win with an ideologist, who does not want to persuade but to guide, who does not want to chat with an equal but to chide an inferior. The ideologist does not want argument but confrontation since he has determined what is true beforehand. The religious ideologist finds the Bible very helpful in this respect. He uses it to prooftext his beatific social vision, which then becomes not an agenda to be discussed but "what God is doing in the world," a mandate to be obeyed. Nothing short of a restructuring of the entire society or even the world will do.

Because of the task it sets for itself, ideology is both insatiable and futile. It must remake the world and redeem all human imperfections, including folly. This is a Sisyphus task, the agenda of the impossible. Ideology chases chiliastic goals with a high self-image, and sometimes with high motives, but with utopian methods and an ancient zero-sum way of thinking. For anything near what it wants accomplished, all of humanity would have to be united in a single quest. It is not going to happen. One might just as well undertake a celebrity telethon to abolish death. But the Grand March described by Kundera goes on nonetheless. Given this, one must ask at this point: What has ideology actually accomplished?

The report card says, not much. As Hannah Arendt pointed out, the notion that all things are possible has to date meant only that all things can be destroyed.[1] The greatest legacy of ideology has been to give people new reasons for hating and killing each other. It has given people an explanation of their plight that has nothing to do with themselves but only with strange social forces and the moral deficiencies of others. It has cut people off from what naturally unites them as human beings—their nationality, tradition, cultures, languages, mortality, religion, literature, arts, and so on—and conscripted them into competing power blocks; men against women, rich versus poor, industrial nations versus agricultural, employer versus employees, black versus white, and even people versus animals.

Christians who have adopted ideology have accepted uncritically the dominant idea of this age that politics is a cure for human ills. This is the General Idea, as described by Hippolyte Taine, that tyrannizes us all. They reverse what C. S. Lewis saw as the task of the good preacher, that is, to take the ideas of Scripture and put them in the language of the age. The religious ideologist takes the ideas of the age and puts them in the language of Scripture. He also proffers a vision of Jesus Christ as a kind of celestial United Nations official, impatiently clamoring for immediate structural change and issuing threats if this change is not made. This is idolatry. But a medical metaphor is better suited to this discussion. In all its forms, religious and otherwise, ideology is a spiritual syphilis probably in the tertiary stage—affecting the entire body.

What will be the outcome of it all? Minogue sees ideology as a statement of hatred for the modern world, and even life itself; it is a "cosmic suicide pact."[2]

Ideology, not physics, contains the key to how civilizations perish, not with mushroom clouds nor with the whimper described by T.S. Eliot, but with self-loathing, rage, and ultimately abetted suicide. Ideology is the social

134　IDEOLOGY: A THREAT TO FREEDOM

expression of a death wish. This, not Inevitable Progress, is the dominant force of our time. Rising, then, for the baleful benediction, a *requiem ideologicum*:

> As it was not in the beginning,
> Is not now and never will be,
> Let the world end. Amen.

RESEARCH EXPERIMENT 1: In your reading on social and political subjects, count the number of times words such as "structure," "structural mechanisms," and "redistribution" are used. Examine critically the definitions of "freedom" and "oppression." Cite examples of argument as described in the foregoing chapters. Note carefully those who predict a baleful future, which they opine can only be averted by restricting freedom. Write to the authors requesting their solution and models of same in the world. Publish your findings.

RESEARCH EXPERIMENT 2: Get to know an ideologist. Assure him you are in favor of the kind of society he dreams about, even if you disagree on the method of attaining it. Together, draw up a plan of structural change for: Canada, Denmark, Haiti, Albania, the U.N., Tanzania, the Latvian Soviet Socialist Republic, Saudi Arabia, and the United States Postal Service. Be sure to suggest structural (not just theoretical) punitive measures that could follow the failure to swiftly implement your proposals. For example, tell them that you would hold back food from them. Send your structural plan to a) your member of congress or parliament, b) the United Nations Secretary General, c) the leaders of the respective countries and organizations. Compare the responses and publish them without comment.

Optional: If successful at the above: a) set up a structural plan for the whole world; b) implement it.

RESEARCH EXPERIMENT 3: With your ideologist friend, select the most unjust rich person in your area, but do not consult him or attempt to reason with him in any way. Let the ideologist determine whom he has ripped off to become rich, then redistribute his wealth to those from whom he took it, wherever they might live. What obstacles do you encounter? Are there any moral or ethical difficulties? List all the tools you need to fully accomplish this task.

CHAPTER 6, NOTES
1. Hannah Arendt, *Origins of Totalitarianism* (New York: Harcourt Brace Jovanovich, 1966), 459.
2. Kenneth Minogue, *Alien Powers: The Pure Theory of Ideology* (New York: St. Martins, 1985), 222.

PART
3
FREEDOM AT WORK

CHAPTER 7
THE ENCROACHMENTS OF BUREAUCRACY

Experience should teach us to be most on our guard to protect liberty when the government's purposes are beneficial. Men born to freedom are naturally alert to repel invasion of their liberty by evil-minded rulers. The greater dangers to liberty lurk in insidious encroachment by men of zeal, well-meaning but without understanding.

Justice Louis Brandeis

While ideologists and their constituents have been busy chasing phantom oppressions, a very large and highly visible threat to liberty is present on every hand—bureaucracy. The ideologist generally considers bureaucracy the "visible hand" of government, the best possible institution for carrying out his restructuring program. Not only does he not see it as a threat to freedom, he often actively promotes it. In addition, bureaucracy is usually near the top of his list for job possibilities, especially if he is a social scientist. After all, how many social scientists are hired by private business?

With this in mind, one should look back at the origins of bureaucratic growth in the United States. One popular religious writer and lecturer faults the church:

> The withdrawal of evangelical Christians from social programs for almost half a century has been one of the contributing factors in creating the huge government bureaucracies of America.[1]

As this vision has it, Christians have abdicated their responsibilities; the government, seeing the result, had no choice but to move in and take up the slack. It is not clear which social programs the author has in mind. While people in the church can always do more, it is undeniable that they have been (and are) involved in many kinds of philanthropy—social programs if you like—on a wide scale: inner city missions, family social services (at which the Salvation Army excels), hospitals, schools, drug rehabilitation centers, adoption agencies, crisis pregnancy centers, emergency relief, and a number of other works at home and abroad. No group in society does more.

Currently, it is government bureaucracy that prevents many of these private agencies from operating efficiently by imposing meddlesome rules and impeding their income with taxes on those who support them. But is the thesis even partly correct as to the origin of bureaucracy?

George Roche traces bureaucracy in history to the plunder and pillage practiced by nomadic tribes.[2] These tribes were mainly hunters and produced little food of their own. When they needed it, they simply took it from early agrarian peoples. Similarly, modern bureaucracy produces nothing; it can only take and coerce. Unlike conditions in the free market, its gain is always someone else's loss.

It is generally agreed that the wild growth of American bureaucracy dates from the inception of the New Deal. In the thirties, there were a number of experiments with central, collectivized government going on in Europe, mainly in the Soviet Union, Germany, and Italy. The New Deal was simply an American version of these. Though Roosevelt was surrounded by ideologists who were ardent admirers of Stalin[3] and the Soviet Union, it was, interestingly enough, Mussolini's Italy that was the model for New Dealers.

Clare Boothe Luce, former American ambassador to Italy, was, in the words of biographer Wilfrid Sheed, "close enough to the stove to see the New Deal being prepared." Of its first 100 days she says: "Make no mistake, it was fascism."[4] Biographer Sheed, a very liberal (in the modern American sense) writer, concurs that Italy was indeed the model.

Fascism is national socialism. The name derives from *fasces*, sticks bundled tightly together with an ax head protruding from the middle. It was a symbol of power in ancient times. One could hardly ask for a clearer picture of collectivism: everyone tied together around a single purpose, a single leader. In the Italy of those days, one saw huge pictures of Mussolini captioned with the words: HE WILL DECIDE. This is, in effect, what national socialism does; it centralizes decision making. It is the opposite of individualism, which is what conservatives stand for. The conservative would take the sticks out of the fasces, plant them in private plots, and let them grow. Both Mussolini and Hitler loathed conservatives.

Bureaucracy is simply the implementing agency of a central government. In America and wherever else it threatens freedom and plunders wealth, it is imposed by government, not requested. It did not arise due to the philanthropic lapses of Christians or anyone else, but was an American experiment in applied ideology. The major model was fascist Italy. This is a matter of record and makes the common misuse of the word *fascist* as a cliché denigration applied to conservatives as another ideological *tu quoque*, a kind of heckling. For example, consider this:

> Perhaps the most serious threat of "galloping conservatism"
> is that in a time of crisis it could easily be transformed into a
> full-blown fascism.[5]

The implication is that conservatism, in normal times, is already a latent sort of fascism that in a crisis could become "full-blown" fascism. Nobel Laureate Milton Friedman, of all people, is used as an example.[6] There have been many crises in recent times; no full-blown fascism has appeared. The only example that remotely fits is the 1979 Iranian oil crisis in which Jimmy Carter, with disastrous results, attempted to put the oil industry under government control. But this is hardly an example of what people like Milton Friedman want. Conservatives favor decentralization, deregulation, and limited government; socialists of all types favor more government action. Historically, they have used crises to expand government power, and hence their own, at the expense of the populace.

Thus the above writers have it backwards. The present bureaucratic system was an open imitation of an existing full-blown fascist system. It is the galloping bureaucracy that is the threat to freedom.

Before examining the relation of bureaucracy to freedom, two things need to be said. There is a distinction to be made between government and the state. Government has certain legitimate functions, and some of these can only be carried out by bureaucratic means, the military for example. In fact, all bureaucracy is built on a military model. It is not practical or desirable to have private armies or a military structure without a chain of command. In any representative government some bureaucracy is inevitable since the representatives themselves cannot take care of all tasks.

However, when government gives way to the state, in the sense of a huge entity that takes over the private and economic responsibilities of individuals, then bureaucracy becomes a serious threat to freedom. If allowed to grow unchecked, the end result will be dictatorship, as it was in Italy. It can be argued that in pre-New Deal times, the United States had a limited government; now they have a preponderant state. This is true in many Western countries where the public (state) sector is nearly as large, or larger, than the private sphere. It is from this state that far too many people think all blessings flow. And they have sometimes had good reason for thinking this way.

Bureaucratic solutions are quick fixes and thus tremendously seductive. There is a social problem, say, unemployment, as was true in the thirties. New Deal ideologists propound their centralizing theories: individuals will no longer decide about such things as pensions, savings, and so on. We will decide, say the rulers. We will take care of you. Soon ground is broken, buildings erected, staff hired, and green government checks printed off and sent to beneficiaries. It is all highly visible. "At least they are doing something," people say, even though their taxes have been substantially raised and possibly their future mortgaged to make it all possible. The pernicious effects of centralization and the parasitic effects of bureaucracy take longer to come ot light, but they do. By that time, the politician who thought of the idea is either deal or a triple-dip pensioner living in Florida, Palm Springs, or abroad.

Nothing can be done by a state for large numbers of people at no cost to those people themselves. It is highly deceptive to speak of free government programs; nothing of the kind exists. Everybody pays, but nobody benefits more than administrating bureaucrats.

It is no secret that bureaucracy is wasteful. The most popular examples are military waste. The Navy has been known to pay several hundred dollars for a hammer or ashtray, which rightly scandalizes everyone. This may give the impression that the military is the only bureaucracy that is costly and wasteful, but that is far from the case.

One could cite horror stories that would fill a book. But that has been done many times, most effectively by William Simon in A *Time for Truth* and recently by George Roche in *America by the Throat*. The reader interested in the mountains of evidence is referred thereto, but one example must be mentioned.

An American job placement plan for people on welfare reduced their payments by $400 million, but all the savings except $22 million were consumed by the cost of running the program.[7] Programs for the poor benefit bureaucrats more than the poor. Writers like Charles Murray (*Losing Ground*) have made a strong case that government poverty programs, far from alleviating poverty, create it. If this is true, as I believe it is—after all, you generally get what you subsidize (in this case poverty)—then bureaucrats are some of the greatest exploiters of the poor in history.

People sometimes assume this waste is simply a question of poor administration, but that is not the case. Unlike private business, bureaucracy is not in the business of making money, since they neither produce nor sell anything, but of spending it. One has a budget to spend, and one spends it in any way possible, however wasteful, or else it will not be increased next time. Bureaucracy is inherently inefficient and wasteful, but the waste is carefully allocated in one sense at least: the bureaucrat is most generous with himself.

So bloated and overpaid is the federal bureaucracy in Canada that civil servants are often tagged "snivel servants." This may seem trite and abusive, but is highly accurate. Bureaucrat jokes have replaced ethnic jokes.

> Question: Why did the civil servant work for an hour on Sunday afternoon?
> Answer: She wanted to get caught up for a month.

Entire bureaus, such as the department of Multiculturalism, are a joke in themselves. Even some Canadian socialists recognize that the Department of Multiculturalism is entirely superfluous and simply a channel for vote-buying pork barrel.

Salary and benefit packages of bureaucrats often outstrip anything in private industry. For example, American federal workers are not part of the Social Security system. That is for the common serfs (the working, tax-paying populace) who support these neofeudal lords. Federal workers have their own superior program. What is good enough for the masses is not acceptable to the elite. This is injustice; this is unfairness; this is greed.

Couple this with the bureaucratic work load—mostly paper shuffling and trying to look busy—the lack of competition, and the inability to fire a bureaucrat without an autopsy, and you have a generous and unassailable position indeed. You are "set for life," as some people put it. In the military, the soldier must put his life on the line when a crisis comes. The career bureaucrat, on the other hand, can stay home, creatively waste your money, and complain about his salary on his half-hour coffee breaks. His solution for every problem is the same: give us more money and everything will be all right. If a program has failed, the agency says it was under-funded or not given sufficient authority. More of the disease will cure everything, of course.

Under present conditions, bureaucracy serves itself more than the populace; it is parasitic. In its current state, it is more than a political and social amoeba; it is like a tapeworm sucking up its host's vitality. The difference is that the bureaucrat can laugh about it all. For this reason, a political analogy is better than a medical one.

We mentioned that the growth of American statism can be traced to imitation of the power-centralizing experiments of European fascism. If anything today may be accurately described as neofascist (with the exception of racist, anti-Semitic groups who openly call themselves National Socialists) it is the swelling federal bureaucracy. Bureaucrats are the "Sinecure Seekers," the elite "SS" units of the system. Like the writer cited earlier who can't tell the difference between Mussolini and Milton Friedman, they have it backwards; they don't exist to serve the people, the people exist to support them. In the process of regulating business, industry, and private lives, they are in effect writing law but are beyond the power of the ballot box.[8] When one is around bureaucrats, one gets the feeling they know this all too well. They know they are the master race of the New Class and revel in their power, as the following example shows.

Based on his military service in World War I, Adolf Hitler received a pension, which he considered too small.

Yet in spite of life-long pleading, the German pension bureaucracy refused to grant him an increment.[9] Even the
cracked Austrian who once ruled all of Europe is helpless before a government bureau.

As George Roche points out, all bureaucracy can do is
implement. Their instrument in dealing with the private
sector is the coercive power of the law. They are not only
insensitive to the problems of individuals but are inherently
so because of their structure and method of operation. All
they can do is create rules, snoop around for their violation,
and assess penalties. So massive are these rules, and so
vaguely are they stated, that many industries, businesses,
and individuals can be cited any time a regulating agency
chooses. This is a form of terror. Employers are like Jewish
shopkeepers in Hitler's Germany, waiting for a visit of the
Sinecure Seekers. Often, an agency like OSHA will have
contradictory rules. HUD once specified building codes for
native American housing that so inflated the price of the
homes HUD would not finance them.

All any regulatory agency can do is follow the rules. If
an EPA rule actually caused environmental damage instead
of protection, the bureaucrat would be bound by law to follow it, pass the buck, or both. One wonders where the consumer advocates are when bureaucrats advertise falsely and
practice fraud. Who protects us when government itself
abuses power? Who cries "Justice!" when government programs both create and exploit the poor?

Many people who would decry rapacity in a family business applaud it when applied by an agency, say, the Califor-
nia Coastal Commission, another superfluous bureau. These
kind of agencies jostle with ideologists who consider the private business sector the enemy. When they stifle economic
freedom, they consider it a great victory. Unable to clearly
articulate their socialist programs and gain power in elections, they exact vengeance through the back door of bureaucracy under the pretense that they are helping and protecting us. Sadly, the public has bought it. These are the pro-

hibitionists of freedom, a squalling army of ideological Carrie Nations maintained at public expense.

Much more could be said about the waste and inherent stupidity of bureaucracy, but this point has most to do with the discussion of freedom. The role of government is to protect rights and freedoms: life, liberty, and property. When government acts not to protect but to hinder or eliminate those freedoms, that is dictatorship. Our present rule by bureau is a form of feudalism that will become total dictatorship if bureaucracy is allowed to further encroach on private and economic life.

Because of its rigid, military structure and parasitic financial support, bureaucracy cannot be reformed, only eliminated. All bureaucracy that is unnecessary for the function of a limited government should be cut off. This is the funereal task of free Western societies if they are to remain free.

CHAPTER 7, NOTES

1. Anthony Campolo, *The Power Delusion* (Wheaton: Victor Books, 1983), 115.
2. George Roche, *America by the Throat* (Greenwich: Devin Adair, 1985), 93-104.
3. See Malcolm Muggeridge, *Chronicles of Wasted Time* , vol. 1 (New York: Morrow, 1973), 254-56, for one of these—Pulitzer Prize winner Walter Duranty, whom Muggeridge has called the greatest liar he knew in fifty years of journalism. Duranty was the *New York Times* Moscow correspondent and faithfully adhered to the Party line. He became known as the great Russian expert in America and influenced Roosevelt's policy toward the USSR.
4. Wilfrid Sheed, *Clare Boothe Luce* (New York: Dutton, 1982), 65-66.
5. Tom Sine, *The Mustard Seed Conspiracy* (Waco, Tex.: Word Books, 1981), 56.
6. Ibid. Sine says Friedman would choose economic freedom over constitutional freedoms "hands down." However, on the page of Friedman's book given as a reference for this, there is no such statement. In fact, most of the page is a quote from J.S. Mill. Elsewhere (p. 76) Sine misquotes Adam Smith as believing in a "blind hand," but this time without reference to Smith's work.
7. Roche, *America by the Throat*, 41.
8. A similar problem exists with judicial activism—judges using their powers not to settle disputes but to remedy perceived social ills. American judges are appointed, and beyond the pale of the ballot box. An unelected body engaging in social engineering is a threat to freedom. See Lino A. Graglia, "How the Constitution Disappeared," *Commentary*, February 1986, 19-27.
9. Robert Nisbet, *Twilight of Authority* (New York: Oxford University Press, 1975), 58, 59.

CHAPTER 8
HOW FREE PEOPLE LIVE

No ruler, government, or bureaucracy has the competence, intelligence, foresight, and sensitivity to handle the myriad of economic decisions and transactions that take place every day. Even a cabinet composed of Albert Einstein, Dag Hammarskjöld, Thomas Edison, Asoka, Isaac Newton, Leonardo da Vinci, Madame Curie, and the all-time top ten of the Mensa society simply are not up to the task.

For this reason all centrally controlled bureaucratic societies—what is accurately called socialism—must be inefficient and must ultimately fail. If the state and those who run it are deified, as they have been in China and the Soviet Union, this only compounds the problem since the Wise Leader is unlikely to say mea culpa when failure becomes apparent. What usually happens is that he blames someone or something else: the Jews, international bankers, ethnic entrepreneurs, the CIA, or even the weather.

This inevitable and inherent failure of centrally controlled socialist societies is not theory but a matter of record. Under the czars, Russia exported food and was indeed the bread basket of Europe. The first result of Stalinist "scientific" collectivization was famine that caused the deaths of millions. Now, with more land under cultivation than any country in the world, they cannot feed themselves and must buy food from the West. The fact that countries capable of exporting food are prevented from doing so by inherently unproductive socialist economies is the prime factor in world hunger today, but seldom if ever is this cited for fear of offending the Great Helmsmen whose plans have gone awry. And of course, attention to such facts would play into the hands of the awful capitalist right-wingers who promote free markets, free trade, and reject redistributionism. It would amount to a defense of the unjust status quo, so we never hear it.

It is also a matter of record that the capitalist, free-market societies of the West are the greatest creators of wealth and producers of goods and services in history. This is true of food and everything else that human beings have found useful. Though even Karl Marx could see this, the modern ideologist cannot. He imputes evil to the free, productive system and may even call it a "grain monopoly."[1] And in spite of the clear record of the last seventy years that socialism is a crushing failure at meeting human needs and democratic capitalism a rousing success, it is capitalism that is vilified from pulpit, page, screen, and podium. It is capitalism that is called to justify and defend itself. In addition, it is capitalism that is blamed for the failures of socialism. This is simply perverse.

Theologian Paul Tillich, for example, called democratic capitalism "demonic."[2] Or consider this state-of-the-art economic observation from Howard Snyder, a popular evangelical writer:

> Perhaps the greatest and most deceptive myth of capitalism is that wealth can be created. It can't. It can only be accumulated or redistributed.[3]

The best comment one can offer is to compare the above with something like this:

Perhaps the greatest and most deceptive myth of agriculture is that crops can be grown. They can't. They can only be harvested and shared.

Ironically, Andrew Kirk, an English redistributionist whom Snyder often cites with approval in his book, has no doubt that wealth can be created and urges this to be done:

On the other hand rewards and incentives for the creation of wealth, and for honest conscientous labor also needs to be assured.[4]

The pressing question is this: Why the discrepancy in results between these two systems, the free and the coerced? The answer is simplicity itself: Only free people are productive; serfs or slaves never are. This is a matter of record.

The only alternative to the coercive method is the free market system.[5] When people are not coerced into working they labor at a profession of their choosing and buy and sell from whom they will. They enter a transaction only when they think it will be of benefit to them. This is the way free people do business. Adam Smith called this a "natural system of liberty."[6] It is simply the outworking of what human beings *are* by creation. In this they share traits with other beings created by God; beavers build dams and birds build nests not because some authority demands it, but because it is the way they are created. They instinctively look after their self-interest, which is not the same as greed or selfishness.

Only in a free system can individuals use their God-given brains for economic ends. No one human mind, or aggregation of minds, can successfully direct an entire society. Those who believe they can are guilty of hubris.

Democratic capitalism and capitalist countries are not the kingdom of God. But the record shows that they best provide for human freedom and dignity, and best deal with human imperfection by separating economic and political power. In short, they best deal with what mankind is—a creation of God with astonishing powers, but at the same time sinful. The record also shows that when human beings under the rule of law and a limited government pursue their interests without coercion, the whole society benefits even if the individual agents intend nothing more than their own interest. There is nothing mystical about this; it is a simple statement of intentions and consequences. It is simply the way creation works. One added benefit is that no man or group of men can take credit for it.

One should add that this creation principle cannot be eradicated even by the most totalitarian government. Under such conditions the free market is suppressed and slandered as the "black market." But even in dictatorial societies it still provides a sizable percentage of the goods and services. Again, the free market is simply the way people unmolested by threats and coercion do their business as equals. The only way any tyrant can completely eradicate it is to kill everyone. Some spirited attempts at this very thing have been made.

Writers such as Michael Novak, Ronald Nash, Brian Griffiths, Walter Williams, Milton Friedman, Thomas Sowell, and others have made the complete case for democratic capitalism; it is not my intention to attempt to duplicate their work. But before I deal with a few current objections to capitalism popular in religious circles, some other comments about the market are in order.

The free market is only a mirror of human needs and wants. Although variously described as "anarchy plus a constable" (Carlyle) and by modern ideologists as the law of the jungle, voodoo economics, Thatcherism, Reaganomics, and so on, the market has nothing to do with "isms" or anarchy. It is really a sophisticated system of information. [7]

There are absolute values in morals but none in economics. It is a fallacy that things have an absolute or fixed value. Marx pegged this value to labor, but his labor theory of value is nowhere accepted, and Marx's contributions to economics are zero. Pearls, for example, are not valuable because people dive for them; people dive for them because they are valuable.

Since there are no fixed economic values, the market tells the consumer what the price of a commodity is at any time, where it may be found, and in what quantities. Attempts to regulate or rig this information, though well intentioned, amount to censorship of knowledge. Those who would most decry this in any other field—academics, journalists, and artists—are often most vocal in demanding interference in the market, which is essentially a knowledge system.

At the present time, nobody knows the best way to deliver letters in the United States because the postal monopoly is protected by law. This also exists in Britain. As Paul Johnson points out, mail is delivered faster in Britain if one crosses over to Holland and deposits letters there. The reaction of the British postal system to this discovery is not to improve service but to call for punishment of those who circumvent their inefficiency by mailing from abroad. Government workers are invariably of a Luddite mentality.

Educational reform is similarly blocked by government monopoly. If a consumer is dissatisfied with public education, as many are, he is forced to pay for it even if he doesn't use it. Opposition to the voucher system and tuition tax credits is pure reaction from a bloated, comfy state monopoly that has clearly failed.[8]

When private persons or corporations—the Hunts, for example, who tried to rig the silver market—attempt to create a monopoly, everyone recognizes this as an evil and cheers when they are foiled. However, when it is the state—which also has a monopoly of force which the Hunts lacked—somehow monopoly is considered beneficial. The ideologist in search of someone to denounce, those "protecting their own privilege and power," need look no further than these government bureaucracies. They are classic cases.

The market is a system of information; price is the point of economic agreement between two equals; profit is, among other things, a way of measuring efficiency. Capitalism (which was not Adam Smith's word) is simply a name for a natural system of liberty, the way free people have lived and always will live as long as they are free. Those who oppose it might just as well campaign for the elimination of typhoons.

In spite of the record of this natural system of liberty in protecting human rights and freedom and in providing for human need, there are objections, particularly from the religious community.

SOME OBJECTIONS TO CAPITALISM

1. Free market capitalism is humanistic. This is an ingenious idea and currently the most popular objection to capitalism in religious circles, for obvious reasons. It can be condensed into a syllogism:

Major Premise: Capitalism is the invention of Adam Smith, John Locke, Thomas Jefferson, and others.

Minor Premise: These people and similar founders of the system were not evangelical, Bible-believing Christians.

Conclusion: Capitalism is not biblical and should be rejected.

Beyond this, it is contended that free democratic societies are based on a falsely optimistic view of human nature as essentially good. Modern free societies are, we are told, a legacy of the Enlightenment, not the Judeo-Christian tradition.

Locke, Jefferson, Smith, and others were definitely not evangelicals. Deism, a theology that makes God a kind of absentee landlord, was influential in those times. But whatever romantic notions these people may have picked up from the Enlightenment, the system of political economy they designed was for flawed humans—sinners, not saints or angels. It was, in fact, a response to abusive authoritarianism.

From the passing age of feudalism and from dealing with the colonial British, they knew the dangers of concentrating economic, political, and judicial power in the same hands. Accordingly, the branches of government were separated, and even set at each other's throats. Mercantilism was rejected; commerce was placed in private hands. They further set up an electoral system that enabled the public to orderly remove and replace those in power. The Constitution protected individual rights. It was, like all systems, imperfect, but it cannot be maintained that it is based on the Enlightenment view of human nature as essentially good. The reverse is true. A read through the *Federalist Papers*, and even the *Wealth of Nations*, discounts this entirely.

If some of the founders of democratic capitalism used their system as a substitute for an afterlife or for genuine religious belief, or practiced the civil religion of Americanism, this does not mean that everyone must do so. I can agree with Herbert Marcuse that people can be enslaved by things without swallowing his analysis whole. Neither America nor democratic capitalism is the kingdom of God, even if some have said so.

The true heirs of the Enlightenment are modern socialists who, often defying God completely and believing man to be basically good, set out to create a "new man" by rearranging the structures of society. Unlike the founders of democratic capitalism, these people concentrate all power in the hands of a few, or even one person. A collective dictatorship is what a political economy based on inherent human goodness looks like.

If any system of political economy can be discounted by the theological beliefs of its founders, then modern religious ideologists are in trouble indeed. (Is the Old Testament Jubilee a "Jewish" system that "denies Jesus Christ?") Christian futurists and those who pronounce loudly on political matters are constantly citing people such as Alvin Toffler, Paul Erlich, and a host of others whose theological views, whatever may be said about them, are a lot further from Christian orthodoxy than those of Jefferson and Adam Smith. In addition, their admiration for Marxist dictators and their kingdoms of heaven on earth is often carried to the point of sycophancy. Because these dictators are, like them, redistributionists, they never do anything *wrong*; they only make "blunders."

The appeal of this humanistic argument is that it co-opts the language of the opponent, the so-called religious right that is constantly referring to the evils of humanism and secularism. It assumes that the Bible provides specific instructions for modern societies. It is both a *tu quoque* and an appeal to authority and prooftexts over results. As one writer already referred to put it: "The fact that capitalism is better than all other systems doesn't mean it's the system Jesus approves of."[9]

2. *Capitalism is based on greed.* Of this idea Max Weber wrote:

> The impulse to acquisition, pursuit of gain, of money, of the greatest possible amount of money, has in itself *nothing to do with capitalism*. This impulse exists and has existed among waiters, physicians, coachmen, artists, prostitutes, dishonest officials, soldiers, nobles, crusaders, gamblers, and beggars. . . . It should be taught in the kindergarten of cultural history that this naive idea of capitalism must be given up once and for all[10] (emphasis added).

Poor Max! If he were around today, he would see that what he described as a naive, kindergarten caricature of capitalism is in fact the prevailing wisdom in religious circles. The problem here is a simple confusion of self-interest with greed or selfishness.

> Self-interest is not myopic selfishness. It is whatever interests the participants, whatever they value, whatever goals they pursue. The scientist seeking to advance the frontiers of his discipline, the missionary seeking to convert infidels to the true faith, the philanthropist seeking to bring comfort to the needy—all are pursuing their interests, as they see them, as they judge them by their own values.[11]

Here again, the critic of capitalism claims special knowledge of the motives of individuals. This is a modified *ad hominem* approach by which the critic attacks capitalism and gives the impression that he and the system he advocates are untouched by greed of any sort. The mere fact that a business makes a profit is not to say the owners are greedy, grasping types constantly lusting after money. They may be, but this is not automatically true any more than Cesar Chávez and teachers' unions are greedy when they strike on behalf of more money for their workers.

As it happens, capitalism is based on free, voluntary exchange, individual rights (life, liberty, and property), the rule of law, and limited government. The system of private ownership is, in fact, a check on greed. In a communal system, the temptation is to get as much of the public store as possible, since it belongs to nobody in particular. The fact that someone owns something means you can't have it; if you want it, you must earn it for yourself.

Granted, greed is a human vice, but it should be said that there are worse sins. Samuel Johnson noted, "A man is never so innocently occupied as when he is getting money."[12] The greedy man harms mainly himself. And if he is to gain money legally, he can only do this by producing goods and services that other people need. This is how a free market society channels imperfections. In closed societies the same person might well turn to cruelty. As John Maynard Keynes notes:

> Moreover dangerous human proclivities can be canalized into comparatively harmless channels by the existence of opportunities for money-making and private wealth, which if they cannot be satisfied in this way, may find their outlet in cruelty, the reckless pursuit of personal power and authority and other forms of self-aggrandizement. It is better that a man should tyrannize over his bank balance than over his fellow citizen.[13]

The greed argument, like the humanistic one, has great appeal because it appears to be based on moral and spiritual premises, as opposed to mere economics. But it too is based on fallacies and should be banished to the kindergarten of ideas where it belongs.

3. *Capitalism is unjust.* Or, as it is often put, "The rich get richer, and the poor get poorer." Arguments such as this come from two directions: (1) ignorance of prevailing conditions in democratic capitalist countries as opposed to socialist ones, and (2) zero-sum thinking; that is, the notion that in every transaction there is a winner and a loser, that one can only profit at the expense of others.

The latter point is the source of most economic fallacies. It insists that no one can become wealthy by honorable means such as hard work, thrift, imagination, and creativity. Zero-sum thinkers often refer to a "fixed pie" which can only be divided up. They believe wealth cannot be created, only taken from some and given to others. It is a bald vilification of human relations. Every entrepreneur is held to be "ripping off" someone. Much of this thinking is based on Marx's labor theory of value, which is palpably false and now finds acceptance only in religious circles.

In a system of voluntary exchange, a person will only enter a transaction when he believes he will benefit. The general rule in free societies is that people who have done well financially have earned their way, and most likely profited many others in the process. The popular idea, first expounded by Lenin to explain the failed prophecies of Marx, is that Western wealth (of the workers, no less) was stolen from the Third World. This is ridiculous. The poorest Third World countries have had no contact with the West. As P.T. Bauer puts it, "Who deprived Papuans? And of what?"[14] Wealthy countries such as Switzerland never had any colonies. And the wealthiest Third World countries, such as Hong Kong, Singapore, and Taiwan, have capitalist economies.

Another irony is that it is not the capitalist but the bureaucrat, whether functionary or ruler, who can only profit by taking from others, since he produces nothing. Only outside of free arrangements does zero-sum apply.

Jack Douglas describes the zero-sum as "the most ancient way of thinking," and "highly exaggerated in a peasant mentality."[15] This is true. The argument is pure nostalgia on the part of the *contras* of feudalism who are everywhere on the march.

4. *The party is over.* "Spaceship Earth is running out of food and fuel, therefore free societies have to go. We must have controlled societies that will carefully allocate resources if our planet is to survive. We have all been pigging out and must stop." Nearly everyone has heard this sort of thing many times.

The predictions of pop seers like Alvin Toffler and Paul Erlich have not found fulfillment, but this has not stopped them from being adopted wholesale by religious futurists long after they had been abandoned by others.[16]

Assuming that we are running out of resources, which we are not in any meaningful sense, can this be made an argument against free societies and free economies? On the contrary, centrally controlled socialist societies are the most wasteful and irresponsible of all. This view assumes that human beings cannot find new resources and will not modify their behavior if conditions become adverse. Both assumptions are false.

The Spaceship Earth set are invariably Luddites. They resolutely oppose renewable energy sources such as nuclear power on the grounds they are dangerous. As it happens, there was more radiation in the air from Chinese bomb tests than the accident at Three Mile Island. More people also died at Chappaquiddick than at Three Mile Island.

The party's over argument is really a scare tactic that has been used many times since the advent of Malthusianism. There is no reason for anyone to give it the slightest credence.

5. *Capitalism gives people what they don't need.* Other critics of capitalism acknowledge that capitalism is productive but say that it merely gives people what they don't need. This could be called the puritanical argument. Generally, individuals are better judges of their needs than collectives or economic sages.

6. *Capitalism is irrational.* Others say that capitalism is irrational and point to the manipulative effects of advertising. But nobody can be coerced into buying a faulty product. General Motors once sold a car called a Firenza in Canada. People quickly discovered, without any help from Ralph Nader, that it was a piece of junk. No amount of advertisting GM could do would now sell this car. Likewise, draping naked models over the hoods of the AMC Pacer might distract viewers momentarily but would not send them running to dealers, cash in hand. On a radio talk show, a caller assured me that, "No one can make me red." If this is true, then neither can any crafty advertiser force him to buy Johnny Walker Red. Certainly a lot of advertising is manipulative, obnoxious, and stupid. In free societies there is always untidiness, but it can be avoided.

7. *Capitalism spawns trusts and monopolies.* Trusts and monopolies are harmful, but can be combatted and broken up. Witness the splintering of American Telephone and Telegraph. But, as Michael Novak points out, why should a socialist object to the fixing of prices? This is Caliban looking in the mirror.

One suspects that many objections to capitalism spring from occupational hostility. Liberal clergy, social scientists, ecologists, and vegetarians are seldom voted into power. They think that with people such as themselves playing Captain Kirk at the controls of Spaceship Earth, fixing the prices, handing out the dole, things would be more just.

But most modern liberals, who are really neosocialists, continue to live in capitalist societies, buy consumer goods, and teach at private universities supported by money made in industry. They also advertise and sell their books, films, and magazines on the open market. They may fly all over the world on jumbo jets preaching the virtues of the simple life, but, like the swallows at Capistrano, they always come back home. They seem unwilling to test other arrangements personally by living in noncapitalist societies. They may dislike democratic capitalism, but seem comfortable with its results.

This puts them in a position that William Simon has compared to a maze.

> That maze, I realized, is the liberal ideology itself—a hash of statism, collectivism, egalitarianism, and anti-capitalism, mixed with the desire for the *results* of capitalism. This murky conceptual mess renders even the most innately brilliant of men stupid. And I would stress sharply that by stupidity I really mean stupidity.[17]

Tough words to be sure, but a gentler version by C. S. Lewis is no less comforting. He also wrote of people who clamored for results and conditions their views rendered impossible:

> In a sort of ghastly simplicity we remove the organ and demand the function. We make men without chests and expect of them virtue and enterprise. We laugh at honor and are shocked to find traitors in our midst. We castrate and bid the geldings be fruitful.[18]

Lewis said the educational philosophy he was discussing, if adapted (which it has been), would mean the "destruction of society."[19] To abominate free enterprise and call for its abandonment, while simultaneously demanding its results, will likewise aid in the abolition of man.

RESEARCH EXPERIMENT: Study your country and community and find something wrong. This should not be a difficult task but if in doubt consult an ideologist. When convinced that you have indeed discovered a wrong or something that could be done better, do not attempt anything yourself. Instead, telephone the federal government in your country, the highest level you can get, the prime minister or president if possible. Tell them about the problem, and suggest that they ought to fix it. If you are able, invite them to examine the situation for themselves. Record their response and calculate the time before action is taken and the problem rectified. Could you have done it cheaper? Faster?

CHAPTER 8, NOTES
 1. Lester Brown, quoted in Ron Sider, *Rich Christians in an Age of Hunger* (Downers Grove, Ill.: InterVarsity Press, 1977), 214.
 2. Paul Tillich, *Political Expectation*, J.L. Adams, ed. (New York: Harper and Row, 1971), 50.

3. Howard Snyder, *A Kingdom Manifesto* (Downers Grove, Ill.: InterVarsity Press, 1985), 103.

4. Andrew Kirk, *The Good News of the Kingdom Coming* (Downers Grove, Ill.: InterVarsity Press, 1984), 83-84.

5. At present in most Western societies the two systems are mixed. Some have called this "interventionism." A society that mixes free and statist principles is at war with.itself. Herein lies the source of many of our problems.

6. Adam Smith, *Wealth of Nations* (New York: Random House, 1937), 651.

7. See Paul Johnson's essay, "Movement in the Market," in *On Freedom*, John Howard, ed. (Greenwich: Devin Adair, 1985), 39-58.

8. Those who insist that the state should fund abortion argue that poor women need a "choice." But this logic is abandoned when it comes to education; any state aid to private schools, tuition tax credits, or voucher system is vigorously opposed by monopolists. Poor parents must not, they argue, have a choice as to what schools their children attend; they must go to state schools.

9. An interview with Anthony Campolo in *Contemporary Christian Magazine*, August 1984, 28.

10. Max Weber, *The Protestant Ethic and the Spirit of Capitalism*, trans. Talcott Parsons (New York: Charles Scribner's Sons, 1958), 17.

11. Milton Friedman, *Free to Choose* (New York: Avon Books, 1981), 19.

12. James Boswell, *Life of Samuel Johnson* (London: Oxford University Press, 1970), 597.

13. John Maynard Keynes, *The General Theory of Unemployment, Interest, and Money* (London: Macmillan, 1936), 374.

14. P.T. Bauer "Western Guilt and Third World Poverty" in *Is Capitalism Christian?*, Franky Schaeffer ed. (Westchester, Ill.: Crossway Books, 1985), 124.

15. Jack Douglas, quoted in Michael Novak, *Spirit of Democratic Capitalism* (New York: Simon & Schuster, 1982), 122.

16. See the essays, "The Dismal Science," "Standing Room Only?" and "A Response to Global 2000" in *Is Capitalism Christian?*

17. William Simon, *A Time for Truth* (New York: McGraw-Hill, 1978), 73.

18. C.S. Lewis, *The Abolition of Man* (New York: Macmillan, 1947), 35.

19. Ibid., 39.

CHAPTER 9
FREEDOM AND EQUALITY

> The foremost or indeed the sole condition required in order to succeed in centralizing the supreme power in a democratic community is to love equality or get men to believe you love it. Thus, the science of despotism, which was once so complex, has been simplified and reduced, as it were, to a single principle.
>
> Alexis de Tocqueville

There are two senses in which people may be legitimately considered equal: they are equal before God and before the law. All theories of racial or ethnic superiority are false; the law should be applied without respect of persons or social status. But outside of these two areas, people are not equal at all.

Gloria Steinem is a better speaker than Jesse Helms; Mark Hatfield is better at fiscal affairs than Augusto Pinochet; Ann-Margret is better looking than Geraldine Ferraro; Geraldine Ferraro is better looking than Imelda Marcos; Jesse Jackson is better looking than Ed Meese. Grover Washington Jr. is a better musician than Boy George or Dee Snider (or any combination thereof); Dominique Wilkins can run faster and jump higher than Larry Bird. One could go on forever. All these people should be treated equally in court, and will certainly be judged righteously by God, but they are not equal in any other sense. The one who wants everybody to be the same has a grudge against reality.

In this respect, creation is unfair; the distribution of gifts and talents and size seems to have favored a few individuals over the many. However wrong this might seem to us, there is no way around it, not even with the most severe restrictions of social engineering or even surgery. No amount of practice will give me the hockey skills of Wayne Gretzky, whose coach once said, "What Wayne has comes straight down from the Lord." What he chooses to do with his skills and gifts is another question. He could have neglected his talents and now be working in a mine in Sudbury or flipping burgers in some greasy spoon restaurant.

Entrepreneurial skills, like athletic skills or good looks, have not been distributed equally. Neither have they been developed and applied equally. Hence, to expect equal economic results is entirely unrealistic. To do this is to totally disregard initiative, discipline, fortitude, thrift, imagination, creativity, and morality. In the main, this is how people prosper, not by stealing wealth from others. If the successful entrepreneur invested time and money making products no one needed, wanted, or could afford, it is unlikely he would get anywhere. For example, who would buy a Sam Donaldson or Bella Abzug doll? The raising of the general level of prosperity is in the interest of the capitalist entrepreneur, not against it. Furthermore, strict egalitarianism requires that we totally divorce people from the consequences of their actions. Why, then, is egalitarianism so popular?

As it happens, equality has a built-in revolutionary appeal that is lacking in the rhetoric of liberty. In today's intellectual and moral climate, equality, or rather the profession of it, means virtue. But egalitarianism, in the sense of a leveling of the populace, requires a frontal assault not only on freedom but on reality as well.

We often read of elaborate schemes for the leveling of salaries.[1] One notes they require a huge number of administrating bureaucrats, who would of course fix salaries at a level somewhat below their own. And if everyone were paid the same, who would undertake the dangerous, undesirable, or dirty jobs? Who would undergo years of difficult training? The incentive would be to do as little as possible. It could only be done by coercion, which means no role at all for freedom.

Because egalitarians refuse to acknowledge that coercion must be an inherent part of their plan, they look to "redistribution of wealth" as a means to equal economic results. The redistribution apparatus too must have a large staff. But if the wealth people work for is confiscated and given away by bureaucrats, who is going to work to produce it in the first place? One cannot redistribute what does not exist.

Redistribution of wealth, we are told, is also the key to global equality. The egalitarian ideologist sees this as desirable because he believes, falsely, that the bad rich countries have simply stolen their wealth from the virtuous poor countries and are hence obliged to give it back. We have already dealt with zero-sum thinking, on which this theory is based. A few words about global redistribution are in order.

In his book, *The Creation of Wealth*, Brian Griffiths explains why redistribution must fail. For one thing, it encourages dependence. If food and other goods are brought in and given away, why bother to produce them? Anyone who thinks human beings will not take the easy way out knows little about human nature. In any case, the good stuff will be skimmed by the various elites, including, and perhaps especially, the Marxist elites. Griffiths also points out that a lot of Western wealth is tied up with high technology; skilled workers would have to be imported as well. More seriously, redistribution would have the effect of reducing the West to poverty by confiscatory policies and the stripping away of incentives.

Most seriously of all, what of those countries who do not agree that their surplus should be taken from them? Will they be punished, as have individuals by socialist egalitarians such as Stalin? As P.T. Bauer points out, a world government dedicated to equality through redistribution would have to be even more coercive and brutal than individual totalitarian governments.[2]

Freedom is nowhere to be found in this picture. Yet this continues to be the dream of Christian egalitarians. On any level, redistribution is a dreadful vision and must fail, except at making everyone poorer. This is what socialist comradeship is: shared poverty and servitude, the equality of serfdom.

At this point one must ask whether the ideological egalitarian, especially the religious one, really has shared, coerced poverty in mind when he talks about equality. He talks about improving the conditions of the poor, but at the same time insists that poverty is the only acceptable Christian lifestyle; the true Christian will be satisfied with only his most basic needs met. He claims to know what people need better than the individuals themselves, and so it is an easy matter for him to claim that these things should be taken away. Indeed, it is a form of soteriology: "Brother, don't be alarmed; we are helping you. We are only taking from you what you don't need."

By this standard, those Third World rulers whose subjects are forced to eke out a living are sparkling examples of true Christianity. These rulers enforce a simple lifestyle unencumbered by microwave ovens, Levi's jeans, individual retirement accounts, Toyota Tercels, and other Western toys.

To make everyone equal in the sense desired by egalitarians and ideologists such as feminists, who even quarrel with human anatomy, would require the extinction of all self-consciousness. In the ideal egalitarian community—the "great unanimity to come," as Kenneth Minogue puts it—we would all share the equality of "drops of water in a clear pool." [3] In other words, we would cease to exist as distinct individuals.

There is another important sense in which human beings are equal: in death. It is a matter of record that death by executive fiat has been the easiest and most popular path to equality in this century.

CHAPTER 9, NOTES
1. For example, see Andrew Kirk's three-point plan, *The Good News of the Kingdom Coming* (Downers Grove, Ill.: InterVarsity Press, 1984), 84.
2. P.T. Bauer, *Equality, the Third World, and Economic Delusion* (Cambridge: Harvard University Press, 1981), 19.
3. Kenneth Minogue, *Alien Powers: The Pure Theory of Ideology* (New York: St. Martins, 1985), 164, 167.

CHAPTER 10
IN DEFENSE
OF FREEDOM

English writers who consider Communism and Facism to be
the same thing invariably hold that both are monstrous evils
which must be fought to the death; on the other hand, an
Englishman who believes Communism and Fascism to be op-
posites will feel that he ought to side with one or the other.

George Orwell

Defeatist is he who, while giving lip service to Christianity
and all the other values of our civilization, yet refuses to rise
in their defense.

Joseph Schumpeter

If one dares to suggest in conversation that, say,
Canada or the United States could lose their freedom or be
conquered, one is greeted with stares of amazement that
soon give way to sarcastic smiles, and perhaps to laughter.
Yet the fact that freedom can be lost is one of the most evident lessons of recent history.

The vast majority of Europe—approximately the same
size and population as the United States—was most definitely not free while under control of Hitler and his German
National Socialists. In France, those who resisted the oc-
cupying forces of a totalitarian power were *Free* French.

Together with the Allies, they defeated the Nazis and democracy was restored. Freedom has its price, and it is a high one indeed.

Historically, those unwilling to die to preserve freedom have lost it. Since a great many people today disbelieve in the whole concept of political and economic freedom, it should surprise no one that they would not lift a finger to defend it. In the church, particularly, pacifism is all the rage.

Pacifists call those who believe free societies must be defended "militarists." This is a most inaccurate definition and a blatant abuse of language. Militarism involves the governing power of a military class and the glorification of conquest. The *fasces* illustrate this, with their individual sticks tightly bound together around the head of a battle axe. Neither Canada nor the United States has ever been governed by a military class. The US, in fact, has a strong isolationist tradition and has gone to war only with great reluctance. It was militarism that the Allies were fighting *against* in the Second World War. Those who believe that when all other strategies fail freedom must be defended and act on this belief are not militarists; they are simply defenders of their families, their nations, their principles, and themselves.

By the false standard, the Swiss are the world's greatest militarists, since every able-bodied man is part of the army, and every house is equipped with an automatic rifle. This is all purely defensive. Now if the dominating ethos of Swiss society were conquest, and if every few months they goosestepped through Geneva displaying their latest missiles and tanks (as the Soviets do in Moscow), and if Swiss divisions were moving into Italy and France, then we might say they were militaristic.

Pacifists like to say that freedom cannot be imposed by force, but in fact it can. The National Socialists invaded France, imposed their regime, were resisted by freedom fighters and the Allies, and were thrown out. Freedom was restored. Compare Japan since the American occupation with Eastern Europe, which is still occupied.

Not only do pacifists deny that freedom can be defended, they may often be found blaring on trumpets that bring their own walls crashing down. Their strategy of appeasement and surrender amounts to a gigantic *Anschluss*, simply letting the conqueror walk in. The "nonmilitary" or "civilian-based" defense will avail nothing. The invader—the Soviets, in the scenario of a vocal pacifist—will simply slaughter as many people as necessary to impose his will. After the pacifists collaborate in show trials they too will have a rubber ball stuffed in their mouth (it makes clean-up easier) and be dispatched by a bullet in the back of the head.

These are the Moshe Dayans of defeatism, charging about with patches over both eyes, penning turgid suicide notes not for themselves but for a whole civilization. If this were not bad enough, some advocates of surrender to tyranny tell us this is the will of God, sort of a Calvinist quislingism. It is a sad situation indeed. As Jean-François Revel has written, this is the first civilization to blame itself simply because another power was trying to destroy it.

There can be no doubt that the greatest threat to human freedom in our time is Marxism-Leninism. The Hindu caste system, the vile doctrine of apartheid, and traditional autocracy are not evangelistic or even exportable. They pose no external threat to freedom.

To date, no country or people that has come under the sway of this scientific, evangelistic fascism has ever escaped. No tyranny yet known in history has been so bad that at the first available opportunity people will leave everything and flee from the land of their ancestors. This despotism, unlike all others, must build walls to keep its subjects in. This is a matter of fact and history, not speculation. It should give pause to those who take freedom for granted, think it is inevitable, or believe it can endure forever without proper maintenance and vigilance.

The ruling ideology in the Soviet Union may now be accurately described as national socialism. Internationalism is simply a slogan; what they have, they hold. It is the Russian civilization that is emphasized, the Russian language that is taught to the many subject nations, the men of the Great Russian nationality who hold the reins of power. As Malcolm Muggeridge has pointed out, the regime represents a kind of slavonic (as opposed to teutonic) national socialism for which Marxist propaganda and organizational techniques are ideally suited.

In contrast to the relationship of the United States to Western Europe, the Soviets have kept the Eastern bloc in their fold and have viciously crushed uprisings in Hungary in 1956 and Czechoslovakia in 1968. The Berlin wall is the most effective commentary on the difference in the two spheres. It is not so much that one is religious and the other atheistic; rather, one is free and the other is not. One sure test is how easy it is to get out.

Yet, in spite of all the evidence, there is great resistance to hearing the truth about the Soviet Union. Because the story of German National Socialism is finished and is now no threat, no one hesitates to tell the world of its atrocities and deprivations. We have the archives, the pictures, the gruesome statistics.

Some of this is also available for Marxism-Leninism, which, unlike Hitler, is still very much in business. A documentary film called *Harvest of Despair* has been shown in Canada and Europe and has been well received there. It deals with Stalin's planned famine in Ukraine[1] in which between five and ten million people, most of them Orthodox Christians, were deliberately starved to death. Malcolm Muggeridge, among others, was a witness to this and appears in the film. This mass atrocity has been denied and defended over the last fifty years by clergymen such as Rev. Hewlett Johnson. When I asked an editor at a major evangelical magazine about the possibility of a review of this film, he asked, "What's the angle for our readers?" He just couldn't figure out why any Christian reader would be interested in a work about the deliberate murder of millions of his brothers and sisters by a system still very much in existence. Happily, the magazine did subsequently publish a favorable review.

A currently popular book is Scott Peck's *People of the Lie*, which has been hailed as a breakthrough for acknowledging the existence of evil, something Christians have believed for thousands of years. What is Peck's example of collective evil? The My Lai massacre in Vietnam, for which the perpetrators were punished. This is a shining example of moral myopia. Actually, it is not so much a problem of morality as mathematics; a few hundred miles away from My Lai, Pol Pot slaughtered millions, yet this does not measure up as an example of collective evil. Why this reluctance to criticize the Soviets or Marxists of any kind?

Our society, in taking over areas of our lives that should be our responsibility, in effect treats us like children. And children have been known to mistake their friends for their enemies and their enemies for their friends. This makes for a most dangerous situation.

One practical expression of this is the absurd notion of symmetry between the "superpowers"—moral equivalence between the West, headed by the US, and the East, headed by the USSR. In progressive Christian circles, anti-Americanism, not anticommunism, is the fashion. To be openly anticommunist is to lay oneself open to being called a "fundy" or "right winger" and associated with Jerry Falwell. This a trendy evangelical, especially an academic at a secular school, can never allow. He has achieved progressive status, hence to be anticommunist would be to backslide. It matters not that distinguished intellectuals like George Orwell, Arthur Koestler, William Barrett, André Glucksmann, Bernard-Henri Lévy, Vladimir Bukovsky, and others have been and are anticommunist and anti-Soviet.

Furthermore, the demonology of neosocialist liberals, Christian and otherwise, often goes beyond symmetry to the point of making the United States the villain, the cause of the class struggle, the Cold War, and Third World poverty. This reminds one of the *Protocols of the Elders of Zion*, a spurious tract about a cabal of Jewish bankers who supposedly ruled and exploited the world. Writings such as this helped to make Jews a scapegoat for National Socialists. Lenin laughed at this and said that "anti-Semitism is the socialism of fools." Today America is the scapegoat; it is held to control everything, to hold an invisible empire. Today this conspiracy theory may be stated this way: "Anti-Americanism is the anti-Semitism of fools."

However much and for whatever good reasons we might wish it were not so, the United States plays an important leadership role in the defense—and extension, if possible—of freedom. It is not the kingdom of God nor the last great hope of mankind, but the prospects of freedom are certainly dim if it becomes weak and unprepared. For all of us non-Americans, perhaps Malcolm Muggeridge stated it best:

> If I accept, as millions of other Western Europeans do, that America is destined to be the mainstay of freedom in this mid-twentieth century world, it does not follow that Americans are invariably well-behaved, or that the American way of life is flawless. It only means that in one of the most terrible conflicts in human history, I have chosen my side, as will all have to choose sooner or later.[2]

No one benefits from supinely accepting the false notion that the gains of Marxist tyranny (and the losses of freedom) are irreversible, even though to date in history there has been no escape. Conditions under Marxism are worse than the situation they were supposed to remedy. It is a colossal failure, except for military conquest, and for that reason all the more dangerous.

The status quo must not be accepted; retreat must be rejected. Though Western nations are custodians of only their own freedom, they should be promoters of it everywhere. This calls for more than just words. This calls for support of those who struggle for freedom. The comments of John Stuart Mill, made in the last century, are appropriate:

> To assist a people thus kept down is not to disturb the bal-
> ance of forces on which the permanent maintenance of free-
> dom in a country depends, but to redress that balance when
> it is already unfairly and violently disturbed. The doctrine of
> non-intervention, to be a legitimate principle of morality,
> must be accepted by all governments. The despots must con-
> sent to be bound by it as well as the free States. Unless they
> do, the profession of it by free countries comes but to this
> miserable issue, that the wrong side may help the wrong but
> the right must not help the right.[3]

While American congressmen debate whether to aid
the Afghans, Cambodians, Angolans, Nicaraguans, and
other groups fighting Marxist tyrannies, an international
brigade of sorts has sprung up in the United States in very
unlikely quarters.

Russell Means, leader of the American Indian uprising
at Wounded Knee, is bringing Indian "warriors" to help
persecuted Misura Indians as well as the US-backed *contras*
fight the Marxist Sandinista government, a colonial vice-
regency of the USSR. Means considers Marxists inherently
racist.[4] A number of revolutions now aim at toppling Marxist
tyrannies (which unlike traditional autocracies never become more liberal) and replacing them with freer arrangements. Some in the West, like Russell Means, want to help
them. He thus sets a good example for Americans of European extraction. His sentiment, in spirit at least, is shared
by others:

> When Christians cease to feel any identification with the
> hopes, goals, and aspirations of revolutionary movements, it
> may be because they have also ceased to understand the
> revolutionary character of their own faith and the compas-
> sion of Christ for the world. Christians too should see the
> reality of the world's appalling conditions and oppressive cir-
> cumstances and discern the need for change of a revolution-
> ary kind.[5]

The Christian faith has indeed shown that it can "turn
the world upside down." It is, in a very real sense, revolutionary. So are the free political and economic arrangements
that have in the past accompanied Christian faith. They are

the exception, not the rule, in history. Free people are the true revolutionaries. They can expect resistance.

If people can be persuaded to believe that freedom is right, just, and beneficial in every sense, then that is a good beginning. But it is only a beginning. One cannot extend what one does not believe or have or practice. We need a strategy against the counterrevolution of feudalism, at home and abroad, whose *contras* attempt to extinguish freedom. All that is necessary for tyranny to triumph is that free people do nothing.

CHAPTER 10, NOTES
1. Ukraine is one of the many entire countries incorporated into the Soviet Union. It is no more "the" Ukraine than Canada is "the Canada."
2. Malcolm Muggeridge, *Things Past*, Ian Hunter ed. (New York: Morrow, 1979), 94.
3. John Stuart Mill, quoted in Gertrude Himmelfarb, *Victorian Minds* (New York: Knopf, 1969), 148.
4. "Indian Leader to Join Fight in Nicaragua," *San Diego Union*, 28 December 1985.
5. Jim Wallis, *Agenda for Biblical People* (New York: Harper and Row, 1976), 113, 114.

CHAPTER 11
STAYING FREE

Monotheism is the thought of resistance of our age.
                                        Bernard-Henri Lévy

Freedom is not the highest value. If it were, as we have mentioned, a prison would be the worst evil. Solzhenitsyn is evidence that this is not so. It is possible to overvalue freedom to the point that it becomes a substitute religion, but that is not the problem that currently confronts us. Rather, it is the reverse: the denial of freedom implicit in ideology has become the substitute religion. There is no longer a belief in freedom as a basic human right, as part of the charter of human life, the flywheel of human activity, and the ultimate source of whatever prosperity and abundance have been attained.

To the sociologist who sees no responsible individuals, only manipulated groups and masses, freedom is illusory. To the religious ideologist, freedom is simply an outworn political dogma, a deceptive item on the agenda of what he calls the "far Right," which, practically, means any view other than his own. More often, it is simply his way of telling the world that he is on the far Left. The ideologist cannot allow freedom because under it, people turn out quite different; some do better than others. That is, they are "unequal," which they must forever be (except before God and the law). The ideologist wants to regulate society until what he perceives as oppression is ended and everyone is paid the same, thinks the same, acts the same, even looks the same, and with one voice thanks the Wise Rulers for bringing this condition about. In other words, freedom must be forever excluded. It is power *über alles* that the ideologist wants.

This is of the greatest possible concern for people in North America. European cultures go back thousands of years and have many identifying and unifying traditions and institutions. Moreover, they are for the most part ethnically homogeneous. North America, on the other hand, is an upstart of sorts, composed of ethnic and racial groups from all over the world. Freedom is what identifies and unifies this culture—as it were, its inviolate genes. North America is the home of *hominus libertus*. To take freedom away from such people is a form of reverse ethnocentrism, which, as anthropologists tell us, is always harmful. Without freedom as the charter of culture, a hundred ethnic and special interest groups are at each others throats claiming, "I was here first!" or, "This is my country, not yours!" To deprive North Americans of freedom is like forcing a Papuan to wear a suit and tie and operate a punch press, or plucking an Indian from the Amazon jungle and dropping him in Times Square. It goes against what he *is*. He just can't relate to it. Freedom is the North American identity; as it abates, conflicts increase.

The introduction of statist—in effect, socialist—principles to North America goes not only against the grain of the culture, it is perverse. It is like taking a criminal who has broken all the laws of a dozen nations and turning him loose in a new land with the expectation that this will cure him for good. It simply cannot happen, and will only provide a reservoir of new victims.

Like Voltaire's Candide and Fabrizio del Dongo, one of

Stendahl's characters, many people are confused. They wonder what is going on, if it is in fact a battle they are in. Of this there can be no doubt. Societies that mix free and bureaucratic principles are at war with themselves. Unless there is a revival of belief in freedom, the bureaucratic—that is, dictatorial—forces must win the day, both internally and externally. If the individual gives way to "the people" or "mankind," and if truth continues to be sought through sociological statistics, we must end in fantasy and delusion; if social justice is considered equality and continues to be pursued through increased government power, we must end in slavery and poverty. If righteousness continues to be equated with pacifism and appeasement, our hopes are dim indeed.

A generation ago, George Orwell observed that totalitarian ideas had taken root in the minds of intellectuals everywhere. Today, when many of these same intellectuals have rejected statist dogma, it is being adapted wholesale by clergy. Edmund Burke, author of the much quoted line, "All that is necessary for evil to triumph is that good men do nothing," also said:

> Those who quit their proper character, to assume what does not belong to them, are, for the greater part, ignorant both of the character they leave and of the character they assume. Wholly unacquainted with the world in which they are so fond of meddling, and inexperienced in all its affairs, on which they pronounce with so much confidence, they have nothing of politics but the passions they excite.[1]

This is not to suggest that religion has no relevance to politics or economics, but that those whose primary role is the preaching of the gospel and the cultivation of virtue are often ill-suited to the task because of ignorance. A glance at the dictums of the Catholic Bishops on the economy or the World Council of Churches on international affairs confirms this.

Worse still, in some cases—say, that of Rev. Hewlett Johnson and his prominent American ideological descendants—these clergy have confused totalitarian political arrangements with the very gospel of Jesus Christ. The New Testament tells us to reject strange gospels (Galatians 1:8-9). They present the political system of some of the most thorough and bloody tyrannies that have ever existed not as something that is merely a good idea and ought to be attempted, but as "what God is doing in the world," and which therefore should be obeyed as soon as possible. This is truly one of the wonders of our age; nothing like it has ever happened before.

Adam Smith wrote of "mendicant friars" who had hindered economic progress by tying up huge tracts of land. The mendicant friars of today are some of the most active *contras* of neofeudalism. These are the missionaries of socialism to the churches. They tie up minds and church budgets, not land. Lay persons need to be equipped to deal with this insurgency, which is a form of spiritual and intellectual terrorism.

Recognition is a beginning, and here things are not so complicated. The Christian-turned-socialist is the man of our age. He is literally everywhere. Malcolm Muggeridge cited the case of Kingsley Martin, a prominent English leftist and former editor of the *New Statesman*. He was a minister's son, raised in a nonconformist (evangelical) church. What Muggeridge noted about Martin and people like him was that although they had for the most part lost their faith (at least its transcendent dimension, which means nearly all of it), they nevertheless retained some of its scaffolding, usually unnecessary stuff such as petty pieties; an excessive sense of guilt; unctuous, emotional rhetoric; and an aversion to art, beauty, and humor. Coupled with collectivist politics this makes a pretty unappetizing gumbo, but helps for purposes of recognition. Muggeridge has noted that every age has its man: Neanderthal Man, Medieval Man, Renaissance Man, and now Socialist Man.[2] Or, as it might be put in a National Council of Churches lectionary, Socialist Person.

Doubtless in the past people's physical needs have sometimes been neglected. But now the reverse is true. The very language of transcendence has become unimportant or even ceased to be understood. The gospel of Socialist Person is body before spirit, like the version Dostoevsky said the anti-Christ would preach.

> Dost Thou know that the ages will pass, and humanity will proclaim by the lips of their sages that there is no crime, and therefore no sin; there is only hunger? "Feed men, then ask of them virtue!" That's what they'll write on the banner, which they will raise against Thee, and by which they will destroy Thy temple. . . .
>
> In the end they will lay their freedom at our feet, and say to us, "Make us your slaves, but feed us."[3]

It is also a version of National Socialist *Gemeinnutuz geht vor Eigennutuz*—"The common good before private good." As the Bishops' Pastoral letter on the United States economy has it: "It is the very essence of social justice to demand from each individual all that is necessary for the common good." This letter was highly praised by leftist evangelicals. Though it was in the main an act of ventriloquism—the vast majority of the advisers to the Bishops were liberals and socialists such as Michael Harrington—the Bishops deny they are calling for socialism, but that is precisely what they are doing.[4]

Once Socialist Person in the church has been recognized, certain procedures should follow. It is not out of line to request that she or he acknowledge her or his socialism, since advocates of democratic capitalism such as Michael Novak and Ronald Nash openly say they are capitalists. Accurate self-description will save socialists and nonsocialists alike a great deal of frustration and evasiveness. If they hesitate to do this, one should have no qualms about describing socialism as socialism and those who advocate it as socialists. Michael Harrington and John Kenneth Galbraith, neither a Christian, have been more candid about what they are than socialists in the church.

Socialist Person must not be allowed to equate greed with free economics, egalitarianism with virtue, or acquiescence to redistributionism with compassion. He must not be allowed to compare his dreams, ideals, and promises with the worst cases of democratic capitalism. The latter must be compared to the performance, not promises, of socialism, which is everywhere a failure precisely because it has been so successfully and thoroughly implemented. It is not fair to compare a highly vaunted but unrealized future to present imperfect realities. In short, no one should accept postdated ideological checks or buy stock in ideological futures, however persuasive the broker, or whatever kind of robe or collar she or he wears.

Since Socialist Person also dabbles heavily in the guilt market, this too must be resisted. If one makes a habit of listening to gossip, one finds that gossips will instinctively seek one out. Similarly, purveyors of guilt are very adept at discerning when their subjects are vulnerable. True guilt is what happens when someone knows he has done something wrong. But let no one accept guilt just for being alive in what is falsely called an "oppressive structure." This accusation amounts to spiritual sadism. Central to the Christian faith is the cross. There, a world's sin, along with its guilt, was put away once and for all. Christ came that we might have life, not guilt, and have it abundantly. Remembering this, plus knowing the facts of economics and international relations, can only help.

In addition to cultivating an organ for the perception of absurdity and the recognition of false guilt, church members might also question how the money they put in the collection plate is spent. The appropriation of church funds for ideological causes is simply dishonest—a form of theft. It will stop only when people become aware and demand responsibility. In the church as well as society at large, bureaucracy is parasitic. Many of the worst ecclesiastical pronouncements come not from the rank and file but from some huge headquarters, bulging with people who not only have little meaningful work to do, but who are both bureaucrats and ideologists at the same time. One of the clearest injustices of our time is the use of people's tithes and offerings to subsidize their own destruction. I leave it to the reader to examine the situation in his own church and decide if he should be concerned, perhaps even angry. If one takes action, expect blatant vituperation and vigorous reaction, since Socialist Person disavows tolerance. The churches need to be decolonized, liberated from ideological imperialism and its chaplains, and thus recover their autonomy. This must be done if they are to be a help, not a hindrance, to freedom.

Perhaps some kind of exchange program could be set up to test those theories of symmetry between the West and the USSR that are the staple of Socialist Person. People such as the gentleman who wrote to *Christianity Today* about Russian expatriates finding a "gulag of a different kind" in America would have a chance to trade places with those in the Soviet forced labor system. The Russian detainee would be able to emigrate and gain what he perceives as his freedom; the American who sees no difference in the two systems would get to prove his point. Both governmental systems would be spared one more critic and gain willing adherents. Everyone would benefit.

We should recognize that we contribute to the problem of government encroachment by demanding services. R.C. Sproul, Jr., in a thoughtful book about the role of money, brings it all back home: "Accepting wealth-transfer payments is a sin against taxpayers and a sin against God, a sin we can no longer afford to commit."[5]

Hard words, to be sure, but such a stance is probably necessary if true representative government is to be restored. Far from bureaucracy being established to fill a dearth of social services, it plays on a desire for government favors on the part of individuals: that student loan for an upper-middle class family, that government subsidy of tobacco crops, those protectionist tarriff measures, that Davis-Bacon Act that mandates union labor on all government jobs, that bail-out measure for a failed industry producing inferior products. As long as that need is there, and as long as special treatment is demanded, bureaucracy will be able to justify itself. It is an addiction and bureaucrats are the pushers. If no one wanted to snort cocaine, drug dealers would soon be out of business. Let no one forget that bureaucrats have a monopoly of force and, unlike even the FBI, can make rules as well as enforce them. The IRS, not the FBI, is the closest thing to an American *Geheime Stats Polizei*, popularly known as the Gestapo.

All bureaucracy that intrudes into private and economic life should be abolished. The cries you hear when this idea is proffered are the screams of economic parasites as comfy and unassailable in their sinecures as turgid round-worms likewise "set for life" unless surgically removed (or un-less the host dies, a distinct possibility). They are protecting their bloated salaries, special and multiple pensions, innum-erable benefits, generous allotment of holidays, protection from competition, immunity from dismissal, their self-serving emotional luxury of enmity against business, their fraudulent hubris that they are helping the poor, and other sundry vested interests. Listen to their complaints politely, then ignore them.

What should they do about work if their bureau is abolished? They should apply for a job, and, if someone hires them, they can work. In other words, they will have to com-pete in the real world of standards, competition, efficiency, and innovation, the way the rest of us do. This may indeed be a problem because after years in a government job, useful faculties tend to atrophy.

The preceeding suggestion may seem harsh, but it is ac-tually a concession. If strict justice were to be applied, there would have to be restitution to taxpayers for the waste and pork-barrel for which their hard-earned money has been used. Application of biblical Jubilee principles would de-mand that the money revert to its original owner. But advo-cates of Jubilee principles seem to restrict them to the private sector.

John Stuart Mill considered it axiomatic that those living on government relief should be denied the vote.[6] With American elections largely a question of civil servants and their serfs voting themselves a pay raise, perhaps this idea, or a version of it, needs to be brought into the debate at least. As long as politicians can buy their constituencies by, in effect, bribing voters, possibilities for reform seem remote. A balanced budget amendment could certainly help. Economist Walter Williams proposes a constitutional amendment designed to protect property and economic rights:

> "Congress shall not confiscate the property of one American to give to another; neither shall Congress confer to one American a privilege denied another American."[7]

It is certainly worth talking about, much more so than naive and unworkable notions such as comparable worth or a government guaranteed annual income.

Beyond these programs and other ideas (such as "privatizing" government programs such as Social Security) lie moral issues. Much of our malaise boils down to the problem of cowardice, which Adam Smith compared to leprosy and called "mental mutilation, deformity and wretchedness."[8] As Friedman, Simon, Novak, Sowell, and others have pointed out, this is a time for courage and action, not cowardice and vacillation. As it happens, this is a place where the church can help.

In the same way that pacifists persuade their congregations to avoid military careers, churches should bring moral suasion on those considering bureaucratic careers. They should be confronted with the facts about bureaucracy, the morality of it, the waste, the way it threatens our freedom, and so on. Perhaps, too, exhortation is due for those church members who abuse their office as bureaucrats, who are proud of living off others, and who flaunt their enmity to the very private sector that pays their substantial wages and double or triple-dip pensions.[9] This is all part of the church's role in the cultivation of morality and virtue. It would not hurt if the church could develop a moral symmetry between the terms *private* and *public*. In the present climate, public means good, private means bad. Greed should also be disassociated with free economics and linked with the encroaching state. These are tall but necessary tasks.

Neither should people in the church accept the notion that the public square, as Richard John Neuhaus puts it, is off limits to religious values. Liberal churchmen were applauded for opposing the Vietnam war and the draft, and for promoting the welfare state. Yet it is somehow illegitimate for conservative Christians to campaign against abortion, pornography, and the insatiable greed of state bureaucracy. These second-class citizen designations should be rejected. Electoral power should be used not as a substitute for Christian virtue, but to maintain a climate in which virtue—and therefore freedom—is possible. Electoral clout must be used wisely and responsibly, but it must be used. Should people be told how to vote? I believe that once people are aware of the counterrevolution of feudalism in all its guises, they will need no instruction at all.

The church can also help to cultivate a counterintelligentsia, which is necessary since mainstream media is dominated by liberal-leftists. This statement may seem extreme, but consider this: Who of all the American television commentators can be considered even remotely conservative? The only one is George F. Will, who gets little air time, confesses a fondness for the welfare state, and thinks Americans are under-taxed. A friend who for years worked at National Public Radio told me the very suggestion that they interview George Gilder, author of *Wealth and Poverty* , was greeted with derision. On another occasion, he dared to suggest that liberation theologians were influenced by Marxism. For this he was called a "_____ fascist!"

In Canada, anyone who shows enthusiasm for free-market economics and political conservatism is considered tainted with "Americanism" and shunned like a leper. This reaction is particularly characteristic of the Canadian Broadcasting Company, which is, in effect, a bureaucracy with cameras. In both countries, conservatives have had to develop their own media.

Christian media, unfortunately, have failed to provide an alternative and, in fact, have imitated mainstream trends and vocabulary: "prochoice," "separation of church and state," "moderate," "far Right" (but never far Left), "civil libertarian," and so on. A prominent evangelical magazine gets editors to leaf through glossy weeklies in search of topics. There are, however, some positive signs. This is also true on the international scene.

More people are realizing that theories of symmetry between the free West and dictatorial East are nonsense. As we have already stated, there can be no symmetry between nations surrounded by barbed wire and nations full of immigrants; between a dictatorship of the proletariat and a pluralistic democracy; between nations openly bent on world conquest and nations who attempt, however fitfully, to resist that conquest. Reinhold Neibuhr comments:

> It is sheer moral perversity to equate the inconsistencies of a democratic civilization with the brutalities which modern tyrannical states practice. If we cannot make a distinction here, there are no historical distinctions which have any value. All distinctions upon which the fate of civilizations has turned in the history of mankind have been just such relative distinctions. [10]

What does all this have to do with freedom? An ex-friend of Stalin tells us what this all means:

> Unfortunately, even now, after the so-called De-Stalinization, the same conclusion can be reached as before: Those who wish to live and to survive in a world different from the one Stalin created and which in essence and in full force still exists must fight. [11]

Such clear statements are calculated to give the ideologist heart palpitations and temporary loss of speech. The religious pacifist is likely to swoon. If this is true of merely existing and surviving, how much more of living as free women and men? If one is not willing to defend one's freedom, one will lose it. The lesson of this century is that once freedom is lost to a Marxist-Leninist dictatorship, it has never been recovered. Contrast this with dictatorships in Spain, Brazil, Portugal, the Philippines, and other places that have evolved into democracies or are well on the way.

Ironically, the same people who decry the whole notion of defending freedom as "idolatry" show great support for class warriors whose struggles are "historically inevitable," and therefore justified.[12] Thus, we needn't take their pacifism too seriously.

The peace movement, however, is right about one thing: the current doctrine of MAD (Mutually Assured Destruction) is immoral and should be discarded as soon as possible. The difference lies in the alternative. Religious ideologists would have us unilaterally disarm[13]—in effect, surrender. The solution lies in developing an effective defense against nuclear arms, which is now technically feasible.[14]

If the development of this defense constitutes idolatry, then the struggle against Hitler was idolatry. It was idolatrous for Allied soldiers to attack Nazi concentration camps and liberate the inmates being worked to death and being used in grisly experiments.

Moreover, under the "force equals idolatry" equation, anyone who resorts to force of arms to attain power, such as the Sandinistas, is guilty of idolatry. But the ideologist has one standard for class warriors and another for defenders of free societies.

As Jean-François Revel, Daniel Pipes, and others have suggested, the West needs to show resolve and cooperation along the lines of the resistance to German National Socialism. The posture must be purely defensive, but effective. We should be strong and hope the ideologists' empire will crumble. If it is a question of outspending them, then that should be done. What are peace and freedom worth in monetary terms? As Vladimir Bukovsky explains:

> The issue now is not "peace versus war," but freedom versus slavery. Peace and freedom appear to be inseparable, and the old formula "Better red than dead," is simply fatuous. Those who live by it will be both red and dead. Whether we like it or not, there will be no peace in our world, no relaxation of international tension, no fruitful cooperation between East and West, until the Soviet internal system changes drastically.[15]

This is true. Outmoded slogans need to be discarded. Our resolve must be to remain alive and free. There are other steps we can take.

We can learn from Orwell's *Animal Farm* that pigs, once in power, learn to walk and talk like humans. Emissaries of Marxist dictatorships have stopped grunting and banging their shoes on tables and gone instead to the Berlitz school of Liberalspeak. People in the West must learn to read between the lines. Likewise, they should be alert to the rhetoric that often comes from "concerned" members of the academy. We will be able to believe that Physicians for Social Responsibility are really that when they set up free medical clinics in middle-class neighborhoods. They are really Physicians for Appeasement.

And then there is the United Nations, what Malcolm Muggeridge calls "that tragically absurd assembly." Here is where the danger of idolatry most readily exists. Gwynne Dyer has made an extensive documentary on the subject of war, parts of which were excellent. Like everybody in the Western world, Dyer has learned that modern warfare is terrible and that a nuclear war would be a holocaust. How then to avoid it? According to Dyer, deterrence, which has prevented a nuclear war for forty years, is not the answer. We must turn our national sovereignty—and therefore our freedom—over to the United Nations.

But have there not been civil wars in history? Have these not been among the most bloody and vicious conflicts ever? A good case can be made that, far from preventing conflict, the U.N. has engendered it. "War is bad, therefore the U.N. should run the world" is a non sequitur of cosmic

proportions. Think about this scenario: International bureaucrats, the majority from dictatorial regimes that hate the
West, running the world. It is ridiculous, like offering to
solve the problems of the Chrysler Corporation by turning
the company over to the United States Postal Service or to
the people who run government liquor stores (the only kind
allowed) in Ontario. All the world a post office or Brewers
Retail. We must reject this nonsense outright.

The withdrawal of the United States, and soon Britain,
from UNESCO is a prudent move, one other nations hopefully will follow. The U.N. has a much deserved low rating,
to the point that when one American official suggested ship-
ping the whole enterprise out, he received widespread support. It may be wise to abolish the U.N. at some future date,
but for now it should be moved; it has been in the United
States for too long. Kuala Lumpur, Tripoli, Addis Ababa, or
Novosibirsk would all be good sites. Why so far?

When loud "ghetto blaster" tape players became popular on the beaches near my home, the noise caused a lot of
disputes and even fights. A law was passed prohibiting all
noise "audible more than fifty feet from its source." Things
have been tranquil ever since. Removing the "heavy metal"
rantings of the U.N. out of range can only contribute to
world peace.

People in the West can also help those in the East to
record the history of their countries while under Marxist dictatorships. The official version simply will not do. Solzhenitsyn
is currently attempting this nearly all by himself. Here the
academic, Christian or otherwise, can contribute. It goes
without saying that the plight of religious believers in
Marxist lands must be exposed and the believers themselves
supported. Keston College in England does a fine job at this.

But it all gets back to us. We cannot promote freedom,
much less extend it, if we do not believe in it and practice it.
When one gets down to it, "Live free or die" makes a lot of
sense. For many people in the world, it is just about that
simple. It may become so for us some day if we do not oppose

tyranny in our hearts, our minds, or wherever it raises its head. We must rid our lives of its shadow. I believe there are grounds for hope.

Marxist expansionism is being actively resisted and, finally, that resistance supported by the U.S., even by liberals such as Stephen Solarz of New York.[16] Religious belief is flourishing in the East. There is no longer any need to submit to the Sword of Damocles of MAD. Vassal states in the Soviet Empire are becoming fractious. As an ideal, socialism is dead, and in parts of Europe one can hear the dirt drumming on the coffin. (It remains, though, a potent theory of power, and attractive for its irrational aspects.) That tower of babble, the U.N., is losing support.

Domestically, though there are still and always will be many problems, the bankruptcy of neofeudal big government is becoming apparent. There is interest in the philosophers of freedom. Young people are more concerned about fidelity and morals. Religious leaders and thinkers are developing the theology of freedom, which is long overdue. For all this, one may give thanks.

RESEARCH EXPERIMENT:
    ¿Le Gusta Este Jardín?
    ¿Que Es Suyo?
    ¡Evita Que Sus Hijos Lo Destruyan![17]

CHAPTER 11, NOTES
1. Edmund Burke, quoted by Joseph Sobran in "Pensees," *National Review*, 31 December 1985, 50.
2. Malcolm Muggeridge, *Chronicles of Wasted Time* (New York: Morrow, 1973), 172.
3. Fyodor Dostoyevsky, *The Brothers Karamazov*, trans. Constance Garnett (New York: Random House, 1950), 262.
4. Walter Williams, "The Bishops' Tragic Message," *San Diego Union*, 17 December 1985.
5. R.C. Sproul, Jr., *Money Matters* (Wheaton: Tyndale, 1985), 146.
6. What of the question of relief or welfare? Brian Griffiths, a Christian defender of capitalism, says that on the question of care for the needy, the Christian "parts company" with economic thinkers like Hayek and others. But the capitalism of Hayek, Friedman, and others includes relief to those who for any reason are unable to earn a living in the market. Hayek says "This need not

lead to a restriction of freedom, or conflict with the Rule of Law." See Ronald Nash, *Social Justice and the Christian Church* (Milford, Mich.: Mott Media, 1983), 55, 56. It is a caricature of capitalism that it neglects the needy.

7. Walter Williams, "A Slight Constitutional Defect," *San Diego Union*, 1 December 1985.

8. Adam Smith, *The Wealth of Nations* (New York: Random House, 1936), 739.

9. Someone I never succeeded in identifying used to drive a government car marked "Official Use Only" to our church. To request an explanation of this unofficial use from such people is not out of line.

10. Reinhold Neibuhr, quoted by Dean Curry in "Terrible Weapons, Seductive Illusions," *Eternity*, March 1985, 22.

11. Milovan Djilas, *Conversations with Stalin* (New York: Harcourt Brace Jovanovich, 1963), 187.

12. Jim Wallis, *Agenda for Biblical People* (New York: Harper and Row, 1976), 113.

13. "Nuclear weapons must be abolished everywhere and anywhere they are. We have called for a unilateral initiative on the part of the U.S." Jim Wallis in "A View from the Evangelical Left," *Christianity Today*, 19 April 1985, 27.

14. See, for example, Robert Jastrow's *How to Make Nuclear Weapons Obsolete* (Boston: Little, Brown & Co., 1985).

15. Vladimir Bukovsky, *Who is for Peace?* (Nashville: Thomas Nelson, 1983), 108.

16. Solarz is much more enthusiastic about the Afghan rebels and insurgents in Cambodia than those in Angola and Nicaragua. The latter pair are much more likely to establish a democratic regime than the former. Charles Krauthammer has called this the "Solarz Doctrine." That is, the U.S. will support any anti-Marxist insurgency as long as it is eight time zones away and has small chance of success.

17. See epigraphs at front of book.

EPILOGUE

Where exactly do we stand? The world is still a dangerous place, and in it, freedom is still the exception, not the
rule. Does a neo-Fabian Age or a neo-Stone Age lie ahead?

In October 1985, a whale got sidetracked from his
southern migration and detoured into San Francisco Bay.
From there he swam nearly sixty miles up the Sacramento
River. So far from his native habitat, the whale was bound
to die if his course were not reversed. Yet for days the creature languished in shallow water, where he was also in
danger from drunks with guns. Now, a forty-ton animal is
not easily coerced into anything, and it is hardly possible to
just pick it up, stick it on a flatbed truck, and cart it back to
the coast. Marine biologists had to entice it with noises and
other strategies.

This went on for days. At one point the animal was
given up for dead. Then he started for the ocean, to the un-
disguised joy of everyone, only to turn back again. The
marine biologists, showing great determination, kept up
their efforts. The press gave the story worldwide attention.
Finally the whale changed its suicidal behavior and swam
resolutely west, through the Golden Gate and into the shim-
mering Pacific where it belonged and where it can flourish.
It was a great victory, to be sure, but richer still in sym-
bolism.

Western civilization has left the wide ocean of freedom
that is its divine birthright and languished in a very narrow,

polluted estuary of state power. It has been going resolutely backward into feudalism, at the same time entertaining the notion that this constitutes progress and reform. It cannot be. With no change in this course, it must perish as surely as the stray whale would have died.

But we have made a turn in the right direction, though like the whale in his indecisiveness, we are still imperiled. Some hard decisions lie ahead. We must choose freedom and reject serfdom. If we do we will not have perfection, we will not have the millenium—but we will be free.

Civilizations cannot be coerced into freedom. Change cannot come rapidly. Like those good marine biologists, we must be persistent and keep persuading, coaxing, hoping, and praying until the Golden Gate beckons and we pass through into the ocean of freedom where we belong, our natural and proper habitat.

The greatest reason for hope is God. The God of the Bible is not the absentee landlord of deism or the vague Life Force capable of advancing our species from primeval slime to level "A" or beyond. He is not the Categorical Imperative of the classroom or some remote and forgotten First Cause. He is the Creator and Sustainer of everything. By him all things consist, and through him all things hold together. He is the Lord of History and even entered it in the person of his Son, our Lord Jesus Christ. He is greater than all the nuclear bombs ever made. Before him, they are less than nothing, a drop in a bucket. It is from ignorance and disregard of who and what God is that fear and despair proceed.

God has decreed that this entire creation, which is not eternal, will some day be freed from the bondage of decay to the "glorious liberty of the children of God" (Romans 8:21). Freedom is eternal.

Let Mr. Muggeridge, a writer I greatly admire and with whom I have communicated with delight in recent years, have the last word. He is discussing our role as God's spies in occupied territory, a metaphor that C.S. Lewis also used.

It has made me grasp as never before that God has an inner strategic—as distinct from tactical—purpose for His creation, thereby enabling me to see through the Theatre of the Absurd, which is what life seems to be, and into the Theatre of Fearful Symmetry, which is what it is. Thus reality sorts itself out, like film coming into sync, and everything that exists, from the tiniest atom to the illimitable universe in which our tiny earth revolves, everything that happens, from the most trivial event to the most seemingly momentous, makes one pattern, tells one story, is comprehended in one prayer—Thy will be done.[1]

Amen.

EPILOGUE, NOTES
  1. Malcolm Muggeridge, A *Third Testament* (New York: Ballantine, 1983), xiii.

SELECT
BIBLIOGRAPHY

The source materials referred to in the notes of this book will serve as a bibliography and will not be repeated here. The following are titles the author feels are of special value. They will themselves provide additional sources for the interested reader.

ON FREEDOM

Howard, John A., ed. *On Freedom*. Greenwich: Devin-Adair, 1984. A collection of essays on freedom by American and European scholars including Paul Johnson and Richard John Neuhaus.

Johnson, Paul. *Modern Times*. New York: Harper and Row, 1983. A report card for the current century, especially those regimes that deny freedom. Johnson makes a case for hope in a free future.

Mill, John Stuart. *On Liberty*. New York: Appleton, Century, Crofts, 1947. A classic defense of the individual's right to think and act for himself.

ON ECONOMICS

Bastiat, Frédéric. *The Law*. Irvington on Hudson: Foundation for Economic Education, 1979. The author contends that statist principles are a perversion of the rule of law and amount to plunder. Bastiat stresses freedom as a human right and gift of God. A brief, readable treatise.

Bauer, P. T. *Equality, the Third World and Economic Delusion.* Cambridge: Harvard University Press, 1981. Valuable study of development issues, the causes of poverty. A seminal work that dispels many popular myths.

Brookes, Warren T. *The Economy in Mind.* New York: Universe Books, 1982. Explores the relation of morality to economics.

Friedman, Milton. *Free to Choose.* New York: Avon Books, 1981. A strong, readable defense of a free market. Especially good on the causes of the thirties' depression.

Novak, Michael. *The Spirit of Democratic Capitalism.* New York: Simon & Schuster, 1982. A Defense of the thesis that democratic, capitalist societies deal with man's imperfection better than any other system. Does for free democratic societies what socialist theologians attempt to do for unfree totalitarian states.

Sider, Ronald. *Rich Christians in an Age of Hunger.* Downers Grove, Ill.: InterVarsity Press, 1977. A textbook of zero-sum thinking and statist solutions presented in religious vocabulary. A compendium of economic fallacies.

Smith, Adam. *An Inquiry into the Nature and Causes of the Wealth of Nations.* New York: Random House, 1937. The book everyone talks about but nobody reads. An adventure of discovery.

Schaeffer, Franky, ed. *Is Capitalism Christian?* Westchester, Ill.: Crossway Books, 1985. A collection of essays by American and European scholars such as P. T. Bauer. A helpful primer.

IDEOLOGY

Kirk, Andrew. *The Good News of the Kingdom Coming.* Downers Grove, Ill.: InterVarsity Press, 1985. Pristine presentation of ideological theory in a religious context.

Minogue, Kenneth. *Alien Powers: The Pure Theory of Ideology.* New York: St. Martins, 1983. Most recent scholarly work on ideology. Not for the timid or those with semantic vertigo. A thorough piece of work, now, thankfully, available in paperback.

Sowell, Thomas. *Marxism: Philosophy and Economics*. New York: Morrow, 1985. Readable work on Marx (and therefore ideology) for the nonspecialist.

For further sources on ideology, as well as a stimulating introductory essay, see Russell Kirk, "The Unnatural History of Giant Ideology" in *Chronicles of Culture*, April 1986. Available from the Rockford Institute, 934 North Main St., Rockford, IL 61103-7061.

BUREAUCRACY

Roche, George. *America by the Throat: The Stranglehold of Federal Bureaucracy*. Greenwich: Devin-Adair, 1983. A drive-by shooting of Leviathan and his underlings.

Simon, William. *A Time for Truth*. New York: McGraw Hill, 1978. A passionately written warning of the dangers of the encroaching state.

SUBJECT INDEX